Atlas of Mind

Atlas of Mind

Fakir Mohan Sahoo

BLACK EAGLE BOOKS
Dublin, USA | Bhubaneswar, India

Black Eagle Books
USA address:
7464 Wisdom Lane
Dublin, OH 43016

India address:
E/312, Trident Galaxy, Kalinga Nagar,
Bhubaneswar-751003, Odisha, India

E-mail: info@blackeaglebooks.org
Website: www.blackeaglebooks.org

First International Edition Published by
Black Eagle Books, 2023

ATLAS OF MIND
by **Fakir Mohan Sahoo**

Copyright © Fakir Mohan Sahoo

All rights reserved. No part of this publication may be reproduced, stored in a retrieval system, or transmitted, in any form or by any means, electronic, mechanical, photocopying, recording or otherwise without the prior permission of the publisher.

Cover & Interior Design: Ezy's Publication

ISBN- 978-1-64560-486-0 (Paperback)
Library of Congress Control Number: 2023951226

Printed in the United States of America

TO
Him
The sole Inspiration
behind all that I think & do

CONTENTS

Preface	9
ABC of human behaviour	11
Are you a morning person or a night person?	14
One brain, two minds	18
Not Remembering a Mobile Telephone Number	21
Remembering and forgetting: Lessons from "accidents of nature"	24
Can you force yourself to forget?	28
Rina's problem of finding her friend's place	30
Does culture matter?	33
Preschoolers' drawing	36
The resilient child: The lotus-in-the-mud phenomenon	40
The beginning of the concept "me"	42
Does introspection improve the accuracy of self-knowledge?	44
Adolescents' dilemma: key dimensions for resolution	46
When personality-takes back-seat	49
The unconscious: The hidden mind	52
Dream: The royal rand to the unconscious	55
The horses that draw the cart of personality	59
The collective unconscious	62
The power of subliminal messages	66
A tale of three personality types	69
Stress-awareness	73
Where do stresses come from?	76
You cope well when you confront	80

When emotion-focussed coping is inevitable	83
Proactive coping	86
Attention deficit trait (ADT)	89
The heart of humour	97
The Lure of Laughter	101
Bronze medalists are happier than silver medalists	104
When describing your friends and foes	106
Planning Fallacy	108
On Loneliness	110
Conquering loneliness	113
The benefits of togetherness	117
Bury your worries	120
Avoid faulty explanatory styles	123
Perceiving control: An essential stop towards successful ageing	127
Roots of achievement orientation	130
The Urge to Achieve	133
Developing an assertive communication style	136
Power of persuasion	140
Rational intelligence is not enough	144
Who is an creative individual?	148
Are intelligent persons creative?	152
Becoming creative	154
Steps in creative production	158
Build your confidence	162
As you think so you become	166
A land of hundred-year young people	169
Will to live	171
Smile and Stay Happy	174

Preface

In recent years, there have been tremendous progress in scientific and technological sectors. This has resulted in a significant rise of the standard of living. However, these advances are not strongly correlated with human happiness. The standard of life has yet to take an upward direction. As basic gap between the standard of living and standard of life seems to spring from the problems of human relationship.

However, human relationship has been complicated owing to an inadequate understanding of individuals own behaviours as well as behaivours of others. Fortunately, psychologists, neurophysiologists and behaviour scientists have carried out an extensive research to explore the frontiers of human mind and behaviour. Yet a schism exists between to scientific knowledge and peoples acquisition. The present book is an attempt to bring together some essential facts regarding human mind and present them in a style commensurate with peoples needs. As a teacher and researcher I have been prompted to take the academic stuffs out of the classroom and discussion forums and make them an essential part of our healthy living. Of course it is not possible to achieve this objective within the scope of a single book. I have tried to focus on some representative areas of science. Hopefully interest of readers would stimulate me further for project of similar nature.

In the context of such endeavor I am pleased to record enormous thanks to Professor Aditya Kumar Mohanty, for his invaluable support in making this project a tangible reality. I am also thankful to Ms. Adyasha Mahanti.

23rd November, 2023 **F. M. Sahoo**

ABC of Human Behaviour

Human behaviour is fairly complex in its expression but simple in its explanation. The complexity of human behaviour is vividly manifested when people behave in non-normative ways. Anthropologists summarize the scenario with some fascinating words. They say:

Every person is like all other persons

Every person is like some other persons

Every person is like none other person

Although all humans display some common attributes and some group characteristics, it is their unique and non normative behaviour which presents perplexing complexity. Why does this man talk in a funny way? Why does that lady lose temper on the slightest provocation? Why does this old man spank children? Hundreds of questions of this nature crowd our minds every minute. Although we may have some ready-made answers, we are not fully satisfied with the causal explanations.

The "why" of a behaviour is rooted in a simple principle of behaviour formation. It may be termed ABC of human behaviour.

First, each behaviour has an antecedent (A) - a

context. The behaviour does not take place in a vacuum. The context may be social or interpersonal in nature. One or more people are present when a person is displaying a behaviour. In the absence of people, other objects or situations may also provide the context. Even a person's behaviour may be in the form of response to the imagined presence of others. When a person is dressing himself or herself to go to a party, people may not be around. Yet, he or she is imagining the ways people would respond when he/she arrives in the party. Furthermore, persons may also behave in response to internal stimulation (some neural stimulation in the brain).

The antecedent (context) provides the stage. The principal hero is the behaviour (B). Yet, what roles the behaviour would play depends on the consequence (C) experienced. In other words, consequence is the director. Depending on the consequences, behaviour takes its shape. If a particular behaviour produces (it is associated with) rewarding experiences, the behaviour is strengthened. The child gets a gift every time he/she recites a poem. Accordingly, the tendency of reciting a poem would heighten. An individual encounters praise for a successful completion of a task, the motivation to undertake more tasks would go up. In other words, the positive (pleasant) consequences of a specific behaviour would make it likely that the behaviour would be repeated.

On the contrary, the absence of positive consequences (or the encounter with negative consequences) would weaken the probability of behaviour. If students find that the class-room participation is not bringing valued outcomes, their tendency of class-room participation would drop.

Thus, behaviour formation is basically tied to the

valence of experiences. The positive consequence that follow a behaviour strengthens behaviour. On the other hand, the absence of positive consequence (or encounter with unpleasant consequences) weakens and eliminates the behaviour. The message it imparts is clear and strong.

1. If you wish to strengthen a specific behaviour of an individual, ensure that something satisfying and pleasant is provided each time the individual shows a desirable behaviour.

2. If you wish to weaken or eliminate a behaviour, withdraw the reward (or privileges) each time the individual shows undesirable behaviour.

3. Learn where to connect and where to disconnect reward (reinforcement)

Are You a Morning Person or a Night Person?

Some people have trouble waking up and they feel most alert and energetic early in the day. Following lunch, they experience a sharp drop in alertness. Other people feel more alert at different points of the day. People experience regular shifts in these respects each day. Psychologists and other scientists refer to such changes as *biological rhythms* regular fluctuations in our bodily processes and in consciousness over time. Many of these fluctuations occur over the course of a single day and are therefore known as circadian rhythms (from the Latin words for "around" and "day"). Other fluctuations occupy shorter periods of time; for instance, many people become hungry every two or three hours. Other cycles, occur at longer period. Many animals mate only at certain times of the year. The human female menstrual cycle is also an instance of this long-term rhythm.

The fluctuations in the alertness, energy and moods over the course of a day are closely related to changes in underlying bodily processes. Daily cycles occur in the production of various hormones, core body temperature, blood pressure, and several other processes. For many persons, these fluctuations are highest in the late afternoon and evening, and lowest in the early hours of the morning. Large individual differences in this respect exist. So the pattern varies greatly across persons. Circadian rhythms seem to shift with age. As people grow older, -their peaks often tend to occur earlier in the day.

The cyclic fluctuations in basic bodily functions and in our subjective feeling of alertness are related to task performance. In general, people do their best work when their body temperature and other internal processes are at or near their personal peaks. However, this link appears to be somewhat stronger for physical work than for mental task.

It seems reasonable to suggest that we possess some internal biological mechanism to regulate such changes. We possess one or more *biological clocks* that time various circadian rhythms. It has been postulated that one structure–the superchiasmatic nucleus (SCN), located in the hypothalamus–plays a key role. It appears that individual cells in this structure "tick"–keep track of time.

The SCN is not a totally sealed clock, unresponsive to the outside world. It responds to light. Morning light resets our biological internal clock, synchronization is required, because our biological clock (and that of many other species) seems to operate on a twenty-five-hour cycle. If it is not reset, our biological clock would go farther and father. This twenty-five-hour cycle has been observed in research studies in which volunteers have lived in dark caves (without sunlight). In these conditions, most persons shift towards a "day" of twenty-five-hours.

The mechanism that governs long-term biological rhythms has also been identified. A structure in the brain-the *pineal gland* seems: to play an important role. The pineal gland sits on the top of the midbrain. It secrets a hormone known as *melatonin*. The pineal gland is connected to the SCN and secretes melatonin in response to input from the SCN. Melatonin has far-reaching effects influencing many structures in the brain and regulating the production of hormones, and affecting many physiological processes. Melatonic is secreted mostly at nights. When nights are long, larger amount of melatonin are secreted. Higher melatonin levels seem to play a role in triggering hibernation in many species. When days get longer, less melatonin is secreted and many species become active and seek mates during summer and spring.

A major implication of circadian rhythm is the concept of morning person vis-à-vis night person. Morning people feel most alert and active in the day, whereas night people experience peaks in alertness and energy in the afternoon or evening. Studies comparing morning and evening persons indicate that morning people have a higher overall level of adrenaline than night people. They also operate at a higher level of activation. Similarly, morning people experience peaks in body temperature earlier in the day than night people.

The difference in alertness and bodily states translate into important effects on behaviour. Morning persons earn higher grades in early morning classes, while night persons receive higher grades in classes offered later in the day. If you are a morning person, try to take your task at that time; if you are a night person, it is better to undertake afternoon or evening assignment. The given box would help you to make self-diagnosis with respect to your rhythm.

Are You a Morning Person or a Night Person?

Answer each of the following items by circling either "Day" or "Night".

1. I feel most alert during the	Day	Night
2. I have most energy during the	Day	Night
3. I prefer to take classes during the	Day	Night
4. I prefer to study during the	Day	Night
5. I get my best ideas during the	Day	Night
6. When I graduate, I plan to find a job during the	Day	Night
7. I am most productive during the	Day	Night
8. I feel most intelligent during the	Day	Night
9. I enjoy leisure-time activities most during the	Day	Night
10. I prefer to work during the	Day	Night

If you answer "Day to eight or more of these questions, you are probably a morning person. If you answer "Night" or eight to more, you are probably a night person.

One Brain, Two Minds

Human brain is a product of evolution. Whether or not mind could be equated with brain may be a debatable topic. Yet, it is accepted that brain is the physiological representation of mind. Although brain is one from structural point of view, its function suggests the working of two separate domains of activity. Metaphorically speaking, brain may be one, but there are two minds.

The brain has two hemispheres: left and right. It has been clearly shown that these two hemispheres take care of two separate domains of activity. The left brain is the rational brain. It is mainly concerned with analysis, logic and language. On the contrary, the right hemisphere is concerned with emotion and pattern recognition. Of course, this not imply that the right hemisphere has no logical and language functions, nor does it imply that left has no role in emotion. By and large, there is division of functions. The left is analytic while the right is synthetic.

Prior to understanding the implication of hemispheric lateralization, another clue is essential. The left hemisphere has most neural connections with right side organs of the human body. Similarly, right hemisphere of the brain is mostly connected with left side organs of the body.

This leads to an interesting conclusion which can be illustrated in the form of an example and/or experiment. Suppose a child is given a bag containing a number of chips of various sizes and shapes. The child is asked to put his/her hand into the bag and count these chips without having a chance to see them. It is found that the child is relatively more successful by using his/her right hand compared with his/her left hand. The explanation is simple. The counting is an analytical work and it is best performed by left brain. Since left brain is connected with right side organs, the use of right hand would bring greater success than the use of left hand.

At the next instance, the child may be asked to indicate shapes and sizes of chips placed inside the bag. In this case, the use of left hand would bring greater success than the use of right hand. The identification of shapes and sizes (pattern recognition) is a function of the right hemisphere. Accordingly, left side body organs such as the left hand generally connected with right brain would be successful to a greater extent than right hand (connected with left brain).

If this observation is extended to other areas of life, there are many interesting conclusions. For example, left ear is more appropriate than the right ear for listening and appreciating music, as it involves patterns of sound. Similarly, left eye is more useful for viewing and appreciating painting as it involves pattern.

At the level of controlled experimental studies, noble prize winner Roger Sperry has demonstrated fascinating results. He neutralized the left hemisphere of a person with the help of an injection and asked the person to describe an accident he/she witnessed. It was shown the person described the accident with all sorts of emotional experience and expression, but the details and accuracy were missing. The analytical brain (the left hemisphere) was not working, hence such results. Subsequently, the right hemisphere was neutralized and the person was asked to describe accident. It was found that there was accuracy and detail, but emotion at the time of description was missing. Of course, these hemisphere work in an integrated manner in our day-to-day life. Yet, schism between the two leads to many more interesting outcomes we come across.

Note
• A picture of brain
• Left brain right brain
• Questionnaires

Not Remembering a Mobile Telephone Number

Nobody's memory is infallible. Yet, there is a marked difference across individuals with respect to the quantity and quality of successful retrieval. It is but natural that people have different types of interests and aptitudes. Accordingly, they display a very high rate of success in some areas whereas they fail miserably in other sectors. A botanist is likely to remember the names and details of a large number of plants. It would be almost impossible for a layman.

Despite such factors of life interest shaping our memory, there is also an interesting element of commonality. When we receive information from the external world, there is a *channel capacity* for a human being. The stimulus, be it visual or auditory, impinges on our eyes and/or ears and produces a sensory impression. But this sensory impression is very fragile. It fades away. The individual tries to process some amount of information, but it has a limit.

It has been observed that seven items constitute the limit. A popular expression used by psychologists denotes: Magic number 7 ± 2. It implies that people in general can remember only seven items following a short and brief single-item exposure. If somebody tells us a telephone number by uttering each digit once in a sequential manner, we can remember seven digits that constitute the whole or part of a telephone number. Of course, there is a variation. The capacity ranges from five to nine, with seven as the average success.

There are *two* fundamental implications derived from this proposition. First, this channel capacity of seven items (such as seven digits in a telephone number) constitutes our short-term memory. We see or hear something, and receive them; neural processing and retrieval is limited to seven. Suppose we see a telephone number of a doctor from the directory, try to remember it, use it subsequently by recalling the information, and then the matter is over. The whole business is that of the *short term* storage.

If we intend to keep it longer for future use, we adopt a process of *rehearsal,* we repeat the items silently or sub-vocally or vocally. The materials now have a chance to pass from the short-term storage to *long-term storage. In sum, rehearsal is essential to transfer the short-term memory to long-term memory.*

Second, the question arises as to whether it is possible to remember more than seven items through the use of some techniques. The answer is 'yes'. It is possible to remember more than seven digits of a telephone number using the mechanism of *chunking.* Chunking means grouping. When each digit is a discrete one, each one constitutes an item. If several digits could be grouped, a large number of digits can be converted into a small number of items. Suppose, somebody's telephone number is 444 666 555 333. Although it has twelve digits the person can very easily group these into four items, each item consisting of three same digits.

Let us examine another illustration. Somebody's telephone number is 19471950365. For all practical purpose, the person would visualize it as three items: the first four digits indicating the year of independence, the middle four digit denoting the year of India becoming a republic and last three digits for the total number of days in a year. Although there are eleven digits, the chunking (or clustering) them would reduce them into three units (items).

Thus, remembering or not remembering a mobile telephone number depends on our skill to chunk or group separate digits into some meaningful and manageable number of units.

Remembering and Forgetting: Lessons from "Accidents of Nature"

The term memory does not refer to a single entity. It refers to a number of interactive systems in the brain. This is illustrated by different types of memory complaints. When a person says "my memory is awful", they can mean a range of different things. Sometimes people mean "I went to the market and forgot what I have come for". Similarly, another person complains "I picked up the telephone and was told a number, but I forgot the number". These familiar memory failures reflect lapses in our very short-term (working) memory system. This system largely depends on the frontal lobes of the brain. This area that malfunctions in patients with depression and in Parkinson's disease can also be injured following head injury and decline in efficiency with advancing age.

The knowledge about other types of memory system has been derived from patients with "accidents of nature". Experts study these patients because it is not ethical to lesion the human brain. Animal studies are also not appropriate as most of the aspects of memory which interest us can only be understood from studying human subjects because of the unique self-reflective aspects of human memory. Of course researchers study patients with memory problems to learn about the disease that affect human memory, particularly Alzheimer's disease.

Apart from the familiar memory failures in very short-term (working) memory system, most people complain of a different types of memory problem. For instance, a person may say– "I discussed many things with a friend of mine last week, but I don't remember what I talked about. I also don't remember who I talked to". This type of memory for events which are specific to time and place is referred to as *episodic memory.*

The ability to lay down new episodic memory and to build a coherent autobiography is essential for our awareness of self. It has been shown that the system depends on a pair of ancient structures deep in the temporal lobes of the brain known as the *hippocampus.* The hippocampus receives input from all other areas of the brain, but particularly from those concerned with sensory information: It receives visual, tactile, auditory, olfactory, and gustatory inputs. It is ideally placed to act as the central telephone exchange connecting togetherness of sensory information.

The role of hippocampus in episodic memory was discovered when surgeons in Canada removed the medial temporal lobe (containing hippocampus) to treat patients with severe epilepsy. The removal produced good results. Subsequently surgeons removed bilateral lobes to treat patients with more severe epilepsy. This resulted in the loss of episodic memory. One of the patients is still alive. He is called H. M. He has been intensively studied following surgical intervention. He is perhaps the most famous patient in neuropsychology. H. M. had surgery in late 1950's and since he has no new episodic memory. He does not remember that his family members have died. When asked about his age, he reports that he is still at his at 20's. He has a pattern of memory loss technically known as *anterograde amnesia*. Although he is unable to lay down new episodic memory, his old memories are available to him.

During 1950's, it was possible to identify the linkage between a specific brain structure and memory loss through the removal of brain structure. Now-a-days the application of Magnetic Resonance Imaging (MRI) provides scientific evidence in this context.

In recent years, there has been another 'accident of nature'. A musician, Clive, suffered from encephalitis. His memory loss is more profound than H. M. He consistently thinks that he has "just woken up". He can't remember anything for more than a few second. His wife leaves room and comes in. He thinks that he has not seen her for years. But unlike H. M., Clive has also been robbed of the memories of his early life. He is unable to remember any specific episodes from his life. MRI scanning in Clive shows that in addition to damage in his hippocampus, he has more extensive involvement of the other parts of temporal and frontal lobes.

The key point in contrasting the two patients, H. M. and Clive, is that separate structures are involved in the laying down of the new memories and the storage of old memories. Damaged to the hippocampus is linked with loss of new memories.

Patients like H. M. and Clive are rare. But patients with Alzheimer disease is very common. The pathology of Alzheimer disease begins in and around hippocampus.

These patients show progressive loss of episodic memory. Now it possible to use some simple tests of associative memory (such as linking faces and names) to predict the onset of the disease.

The third types of memory failure involve semantic memory. When a person cannot remember the name of an object (say a hammer), the type of memory loss is called loss of semantic memory. One of the most significant development in understanding the loss of semantic memory has occurred in the 1980's. Experts come across a rare disorder known as "semantic dementia". In semantic dementia, there is progressive erosion of the database. Patients are unable to name objects and understand meaning of words and objects. These deficits are more apparent in language, but can also be demonstrated on visual tests.

More recently, it has been shown that the right temporal lobe seems to play a particular role in the storage of knowledge about people while left side of the temporary lobe is involved in the loss of knowledge for nonliving things. Thus, semantic memory for living and man made things seem to be segregated.

Can you Force Yourself to Forget?

All of us have memories we'd prefer to forget. When we have experience of positive events, we tend to store and retrieve memories. When negative events are encountered, we try sometimes to forcefully to forget such experiences. We suggest to ourselves: forget. During hours of consolation, others also follow the same technique of suggesting: "Please forget the event". The fundamental question concerns: Does it work?

It was the noted psychologist, Sigmund Freud, who spoke of this kind of forgetting. According to Freud, unpleasant memories disturb the stability of the ego. Accordingly, people force their memories into the realm of the unconscious.

However, many psychologists do not agree with Freud. Some of the critics argue that there is no objective proof supporting the existence of the unconscious. These critics cite the rule that there is an equal and opposite reaction to every action. If we try to force us to forget something, the materials gain strength. As a result, these are better remembered.

Interestingly, the controversy has reached a new dimension with the advent of modern and technologically advanced techniques of studying brain functions. In recent years, it is possible to specify the specific brain centres that are linked with particular activities. As every body knows, specific brain centres are concerned with auditory functions. Although these are previously known facts, the centres for relatively more complex functions such as solving mathematical problems can now be identified with the application of magnetic resonance methods.

With the application of magnetic resonance techniques, neurologists have observed brain function at the time of people's remembering and forgetting unpleasant experiences. People are advised to think of unpleasant events while comparable group of people are advised to forget unpleasant events. This think/nothink design reveals an interesting finding.

It is shown that hippocampus-a centre of the brain linked with memory-is activated when people remember unpleasant event. On the contrary, another centre which is linked with memory-inhibitory functions is shown to be active while people try to forget.

The message of the finding is clear. When people try to forget unpleasant events, the efforts do not go waste. The self-suggestion prompting "forget" seems to work. Parenthetically it is also suggested that relatives and social workers who offer counselling to the agonized victims do help in reducing the agony if they say – "please, forget the awful event".

Rina's Problem of Finding her Friend's Place

Rina has been driving her private car for quite some years. She is also not an introverted personality. She drives a lot and moves out a lot. Yet, she encounters frequent problems of locating her friends' place accurately and timely. She also makes error in parking her car. Her folks are worried, yet problem continues.

Looking at Rina's problem, many people would hasten to add that Rina is not a solitary case. This problem is common with girls and women. Is there any scientific validity for this assertion?

The scientific research on the question of spatial-visual ability clearly shows a male advantage. Of course, the gap between men and women with respect to spatial-visual ability is gradually being narrowed. Yet, a gap exists and women demonstrate poorer spatial-visual ability compared with men. There may be exceptional cases where women surpass. But men surpass woman on the skills of spatial-visual nature.

Although girls and women perform as well on standard intelligence tests at par with boys and men, component-wise analysis shows that boys and men perform better on picture assembly and figure puzzle. These subtests are indicators of spatial-visual ability.

However, the fundamental question involves: Why? At an analytical level the answer could be offered in terms of neurological (physiological) terms. It is accepted that specific neural centres of the brain are responsible for particular functions. Just as there are specific brain centres for our visual function, there are also particular centres for spatial-visual perception. It could be argued that such centres are more developed in man than in woman's brain.

Although the explanation sounds reasonable, another question of deeper level arises. How did this difference originate in the first place?

Brain is not a static and unchanged structural entity. In the process of evolution, it has changed. It has also changed in response to altering environmental conditions. Accordingly, evolutionary psychologists have provided a satisfactory explanation in this context.

According to evolutionary psychologists, life started differently for men and women. At the primitive stage, males were basically hunters. Females were basically fruit-gatherers. This induced a change at the neurophysiological level.

The activity of hunting surely required adaptive skills of spatial nature. If hunters can not discriminate various textures of land, it would spell danger for them. For hunting and fishing effectively, one needs to have good spatial-visual discrimination. Discrimination of various types of trees, identification of different forms of flora and fauna, assessment of distance and evaluation of sizes and shapes are functional aspect of a hunter. Thus, hunters had to develop spatial visual ability for their survival and adaptation. It facilitated the growth of spatial centres in male brain. Females, on the contrary, were concerned with fruit gathering. Accordingly, the brain was equipped with location memory.

This analysis from evolutionary point of view clearly suggests the explanation of males' superior spatial skill. The same explanation further suggests that the gap is decreasing because women are now accepting new roles. The scientific evidence has also clearly shown that the male advantage with respect to spatial skill is not as pronounced these days as it was in the past.

Does Culture Matter?

When you look at the picture on the computer screen at night, where do you eyes linger longer? Surprisingly, the answer to this question might differ depending upon where you were raised. Westerners stare more at the train in the center while easterners let their eyes roam more around the entire picture.

The difference reflects more general divide between westerners and easterners. People's cultural background affects their cognitive processes, categorization, learning, causal reasoning, and even attention and perception.

Asians whose more collectivist culture promotes group, group harmony and contextual understanding of situation think in a more holistic way. They pay attention to all the elements of a scene, to context and to the relationship between items. Western culture, in contrast, emphasizes personal autonomy and formal logic. Accordingly, westerners are more analytic and pay attention to particular objects and categories.

In a recent study, a research used a tracking device to monitor the eye movement of 25 American and 27 Chinese graduate students. The students stared for three seconds at pictures of objects against complex background. The 36 pictures included a train, a tiger in a forest and an aeroplane with mountains in the background. The researcher found that Americans focused on the foreground object 118 milliseconds sooner than the Chinese participants did and then continued to look at the focal object longer. The Chinese tended to move their eyes back and forth more between the main object and the background and looked at the background for longer than the Americans did.

In a similar study, a researcher showed Japanese and American participants animated underwater vignettes that included three big fish and background objects like rocks, seaweed and water bubbles. When participants were asked to describe the scenes, Americans were more likely to begin by recalling the focal fish. In contrast, Japanese were likely to describe the whole scene, saying something like "It was a lake or pond" Later the Japanese participants all recalled more details about the background objects than the Americans did. Americans immediately zoomed in the objects. The Japanese pay more attention to context.

Cognitive differences between Westerners and Asians show up in other areas as well. For example, in tests of categorization, Americans are more likely to group items fit into categories by type. For example, a cow and a dog may go together, because these are animals. Asians are likely to group items based on relationship. So a cow and grass might go together because cow eats grass.

Another difference between Westerners and Easterners regards fundamental explanatory styles. It is believed that people generally overemphasize personality-related explanation for others behaviour while underemphasizing or ignoring contextual (situational) factors. For example, a man may believe he tripped and fell because of a crack in the footpath, but assume that someone else fell because of clumsiness. However, Asians are much more likely to consider contextual factors while trying to explain other people's behaviour. In an analysis of American and Chinese newspaper account of murders, a difference is found. American reporters emphasize the personal attributes of the murders, while Chinese reporters emphasize more on situational factors.

Why these differences occur is not fully explained. Yet, it appears that cognitive differences come from social differences. There is a place in Japan where life style is predominantly American. It is Hokkaido, called Japan's "Wild West". It is shown that residents of Hokkaido exhibit cognitive style characteristic of Americans.

Since the socio-cultural context matters, it is useful to "recognize" the multiplicity of thinking style. In a recent survey, European-American and first-generation Asian-American were given a series of complex logical problems to solve. Some participants solved the problem silently, while others had to talk out loud and explain their reasoning as they worked. It was found that European Americans who talked out loud solved the problem just as well as those who stayed silent. But being forced to talk seriously undermined the Asian students' performance. In general Asians may think and reason in a less readily "verbalizable" way than Westerners. For Asians, it is more intuitive and less linear. In such a context. It is important to recognize that certain aspects of thinking are universal and certain aspects are culture-specific.

Preschoolers' Drawing

Children's drawing represent fine motor coordination. Not all motor activities of young children involve the strength, agility, and balance of their whole bodies. Many require the coordination of small movements but not strength. One widespread fine motor skill is drawing. Every young child tries using pens or pencils at sometime. The scribbles or drawings that result probably serve a number of purposes. At times they may be used mainly for sensory exploration. A child may get to the feel of tip of the pen. At other times, drawings may express thoughts or feelings. A child may suggest this possibility by commenting, "It's a house". Children's drawing also probably reflect their knowledge of the world, even though they may not yet have the finer motor skill they need to convey their knowledge fully. In other words, children's drawings reveal not only fine motor coordination but their self-concept, emotional and social attitudes, and cognitive development.

Drawing shows two overlapping phases of development during the preschool period. From the ages of two and one-half to four, children focus on developing prerepresentational skills, such as scribbling and the purposeful drawings of simple shapes and designs. Sometimes around age four, they begin attempting to represent objects. Although representational drawings usually follow prerepresentational ones, the two types stimulate each other simultaneously

Prerepresentational Drawings. Around the end of infancy, children begin to scribble. A two-year-old experiments with whatever pen or pencil is available to him/her. In doing so, they behave like infants and like children. As infants their efforts focus primarily on the activity itself on the motion and sensation of handling a pen or a pencil. But like an older child, two-year-olds often care about the outcome of those activities. "That's a Mommy", it says, whether it looks like one or not. Contrary to a popular view of children's art, even very young children are concerned not only with the process of drawing but with the product as well.

Representational Drawings. While preschool children improve their scrabbling skills, they also develop an interest in representing people, objects, and events in their drawings. This interest often far precedes their ability to do so. A three-year-old may assign meanings to scribbles. During the preschool years, and for a long time thereafter the child's visual representations are limited by his/her comparatively rudimentary fine motor skills. Apparently he/she knows more, visually speaking, than his/her hands can portray with a pen or pencil. Given an outline of a person and some contours or body parts (nose, mouth, eyes, and so on), a preschooler can assemble a human being quite skillfully. The preschooler can put most of the parts where they ought to go. But given a pencil and a paper, a young preschooler may still produce only a rudimentary drawing of a person–a circle with dots for eyes and sticks for legs. Only as the child reaches school age, drawings become relatively realistic.

Rhoda Kellogg, a creative teacher of preschool children has been observing young children's artistic efforts for many decades. She has assembled an impressive array of tens of thousands of drawings produced by more than 2000 preschool children. Kellogg has shown that young children's artistic productions are orderly, meaningful and structured.

By their second birthday, children can scribble. Scribbles represent the earliest forms of drawing. Every form of graphic art, no matter how complex, contains the lines found in children's art work, which Kellogg calls the twenty basic scribbles. These include vertical, horizontal, diagonal, circular, curving, waving or zigzag lines, and dots. As young children progress from scribbling to picture making, they go through four distinguishable stages: placement, shape, design and pictorial.

The *placement stage* is Kellogg's term for 2 to 3 years olds' drawings, drawn on a page in a placement pattern. One example of these patterns is the spaced border pattern. The *shape stage* is Kellogg's term for 3- year-olds drawing consisting of diagrams in different shapes. Young children draw basic six shapes–circle, square, rectangle, triangles, crosses, Xs, and forms. The *design stage* is Kellogg's term for 3 to 4-year-of-olds drawing in which young children mix two basic shapes into a more complex design. The *pictorial stage* is Kellogg's term for 4 to 5-year-of-old's drawings which consist of objects that adult can recognize.

Young children often use some formula for drawing different things. Though modified in small ways, one basic form can cover a range of objects. When children begin to draw animals, they portray them in the same way they portray humans, standing upright with a smiling face, legs, and arms. Pointed ears may be the only clue adults have as to the nature of the particular beast. As children become more aware of the nature of a cat, their drawings acquire more cat-like features.

The Resilient Child: The Lotus-in-the-mud Phenomenon

Environment makes the man, so says commonsense. It is true that the beauty of the environment is reflected in the decency of behaviour of people the environment produces. An environment that offers ample and equitable opportunity for individual as well as for collective growth is required to be maintained and promoted. But what about the impoverished environment?

It is also found that impoverished environment produces negative consequences. Many children who are reared in slims and disadvantaged homes develop antisocial behaviour. Children in such crime-prone environment show systems of criminal behaviours.

Despite such association between adverse circumstances and disruptive behaviours, a surprise finding is a group of children who prevent and minimize the negative consequences. These children are called *resilient (invulnerable) children*. They represent the lotus-in-the-mud phenomenon. In the West, it has been estimated that 30 percent of children brought up in slums indicate such invulnerability.

A significant proportion of research has been

undertaken to delineate conditions that foster resilience. The most important finding pertains to the significant role of *protective factors*. It has been shown that resilient children do have the special mechanism of their need satisfaction. In their desert-like environment, there is always an oasis -a significant other whose protection they secure. Such a sympathetic and empathetic significant other may be a friend or a teacher or a relative or any other adult in their Environment-Alternatively, it could be a small collectively such as club, temple, school or any small organization. At the time of success, the child first reports his/her achievement to this person. At the time of failure and adversity, the child confides his/her feeling, to such individual. The child opens his/her heart to this person prior to bringing any news (good or bad) to his family and parents. Of course, parents or one of the parents may provide such unusual bonding.

In addition to such special mode of need gratification through special protective factor, the resilience child is successful in developing three kinds of resources: *I am, I have, and I can*.

A strong source of the invulnerability involves the child's sense of positive self-concept. Such children believe that they love others and others love them too. They also believe that they have many good qualities. They have a sense of self-worth.

Second, these children believe that they have people to depend on. They have persons who would help them at the time of need. Finally, these children have a sense of self-efficacy. They believe that they can execute a function competently. They can solve problems and they can also understand their limitations.

The Beginning of the Concept "Me"

The beginning of the concept "me" provides useful clues to our understanding of ourselves. Except for human beings, only great apes–chimpanzees, gorillas, and orangutans–seem capable of self–recognition. A psychologist placed different species of animals in a room with a large mirror. At first, they greeted their own images by vocalizing, gesturing, and making other social responses. After several days, the great apes–but not the other animals–began to use the mirror to pick food out of their teeth, groom themselves, blow bubbles, and make faces for their entertainment. From all appearances, they recognized themselves.

In other studies, the investigator anesthetized the animals, then painted an odourless red dye on their brows, and returned them to mirror. On seeing the red spot, only the apes reached their brows. This proved that they perceived the image as their own. By using a similar red dye test, child psychologists have found that most human infants begin to recognize themselves in the mirror between the ages of eighteen and twenty-four months. It is believed that self-recognition among great apes and human infants is the first clear expression of the concept "me".

The ability to see yourself as a distinct entity is a necessary first step in the evolution and development of a *self-concept*, the sum total of beliefs you have and can communicate about yourself. The second step involves social factors. Sociologists have introduced the term *looking-glass self* to suggest the people serve as mirror in which we see ourselves. They argue that we often come to know ourselves by imagining what significant others think of us. We then incorporate these perceptions into our self-concepts. It is interesting that those that had been raised in isolation-without exposure to peers –did not recognize themselves in the mirror. Only after such exposure did they begin to show signs of self-recognition.

Although sociologists argue in favour of a match between our self-concepts and our perceptions of what others think of us, this is not always so. What we think of ourselves do not match what specific others actually think of us. In other words, there are other sources that contribute towards the formulation of self-concept.

Does Introspection Improve the Accuracy of Self-Knowledge?

How do people achieve insights into their own beliefs, attitudes, emotions and motivation? Whether the prescribed technique is meditation, psycho-therapy, religion, dream analysis or hypnosis, the advice is basically the same. Self-knowledge is derived from introspection, a looking inward at one's own thoughts and feelings.

An investigation interviewed college students and asked them to discuss their social relationship, career goals, important life decisions, conflicts and other personal topics. Before the interview, the participants were instructed to focus on their thoughts and feelings or their overt behaviour or a mixture of both. Afterwards, participants who had described their thoughts and feelings rated their interviews as more informative about themselves than did those who had focused only on behaviour. Independent observers (who were strangers to the participants) felt the same way.

Too much introspection can also impair certain type of judgments. It is said that under some circumstances, analysis is paralysis. In a study, people were asked to taste and rate five brands of jam. Those who were asked to list the reasons for their taste preference agreed less with *consumer reports* experts than did those who made their ratings without analysis. Apparently, it is possible to think too much only to get confused.

Is introspection futile? Not necessarily. People generally reflect on their behaviour by listing either *reasons or feelings*. Whether this reflection provides valuable insight depends on whether the behaviour in question is caused more by cognitive or affective factors, thoughts or feelings. For behaviours that are cognitively driven, such as making business investment decisions, a listing of reasons may well increase the accuracy of self-knowledge but for behaviours that are affectively determined, such as romantic relationship, it may not. To determine why you love a person or enjoy a work of art, focusing on your feelings is more helpful than making a list of reasons.

The usefulness of introspection may also depend on the amount of time people have and the cognitive resources available. Cognitive resources imply the availability of multiple dimensions. If a person introspects on the issue of his/her business. It is necessary that he/she is familiar with a number of aspects (dimensions) of business. Without such cognitive resources, analysis may not be effectively carried out. Thus, introspection can increase self-insight provided that we have enough time and cognitive resources.

Adolescents' Dilemma: Key Dimensions for Resolution

'To be or not to be' is a basic dilemma in all of us. It is not a dilemma and confined to only Hamlet. During all stages of life, we encounter dilemma of one kind or the other. Erikson has rightly depicted human development as a series of conflict resolution. Although Freud believed that the conflicts are rooted in the biological constitution of man, Erikson stressed the social component of the problem.

According to Erikson, an infant (birth to one year) encounters the conflict between trust and mistrust. If its needs are appropriately looked after, the child develops a sense of trust. In contrast, the lack of sensitive and appropriate care-giving activities leads to the induction of mistrust in the child. Similarly, the conflict during early childhood (one to three years of age) centres around autonomy and shame while the conflict during middle childhood (three to six years of age) is linked with initiative and guilt. Subsequently, the late childhood (six to twelve years of age) presents conflict between industry and inferiority.

During adolescence, the biological changes and hormonal growth-stimulates self-consciousness. The kind of conflict that characterizes this period pertains to his/her role as a being. The adolescent encounters the conflict between *role identity* and *role confusion*. Would he/she model his/her parents? What would be the appropriate vocation/profession during next phase of life? What are the values and goals that are appropriate for him/her? What kind of preparation is needed at his/her and? These are some of the fundamental questions that bother adolescents.

The resolution of this conflict not only curb the stress and strain that characterizes adolescent period, the resolution prepares a smooth ground for successful transition to pre-adult phase. In contrast, the continuation of the conflict for prolonged period generates problems. The adolescent revolts against the socialization process. The relationship with parents becomes problematic. Out of frustration, adolescents are likely to manifest a number of disruptive behaviours such as drug addition, alcoholism and antisocial behaviours.

It has been observed that the resolution attempts may take four different forms. The two key dimensions in the resolution process involve *commitment* and *decisiveness*. Let us consider the case of Rina. Rina is now studying in high school. She has already decided that she would go for Engineering degree later in a professional college. Accordingly, she attaches weight to her academic subjects and studies diligently so that she would be successful later. She has a high level of personal commitment. This style that blends a high level of commitment and decisiveness is very adaptive. It is called *identity achievement*.

Kamal represents another style. He is very obedient. He knows that his father is running a big business. As soon as Kamal completes his basic education, he would be able to join his father's business. He has no hesitation. He does not have to weigh several alternatives as the goal has been already set for him. In this case, there is no need for decision making. It is likely that Kamal would have no difficulty in business. This style can be described as *foreclosure commitment without crisis*.

Ranjit has no serious attitude. He is studying alright. He thinks that he would try to fit with any scope that comes in his way. He is not worried. He believes that he would love the job that would come his way. Though there is decisiveness, there is also partial commitment. They are seemingly care-free people who have actively avoided commitment. The style is termed *identity diffusion*.

Mina has not yet made a decision about her life goals. She is agonizing over them. She thinks that she may be interested in something having to do with science, but she is torn between a medical programme and engineering school. This style can be described as moratorium in crisis.

The categorization process indicates that the key-factors in resolution of identity crisis include commitment and decisiveness. Of these two dimensions, commitment plays an important role. Adolescents who are trained to develop commitment put themselves on the road to successful resolution of conflict.

Identity Styles	Decisiveness in considering alternatives	Commitment (Adherence to a path or action)
Identity Achievement	Present	Present
Foreclosure	Absent	Present
Identity Diffusion	Present or absent	Absent
Moratorium	In crisis	Present but vague

When Personality Takes Back Seat

Can behaviour be predicted on the basis of one's personality? Many people think 'yes'. If not, why should we waste time and energy in analyzing and assessing one's personality. If we know a person to be extrovert, we expect him or her to be garrulous in a party. If we know someone as introvert, we anticipate his or her absence in a huge gathering. Although personality labels help us to classify people into broad categories and predict their probable behaviour, the task is not as simple as we think.

In fact there are conditions when personality loses its decisive influence. Sometimes we face an interesting question: Which is important situation or the personality?

A satisfactory answer to this question involves a conditional statement. If situation is structured (or clear), situation determines behaviour. If situation is unstructured (unclear), the personality plays a major role. In other words, personality-takes a back seat under condition of clarity.

Think of a wedding reception. This is a situation where many conditions are structured. Guests are expected to arrive at a particular time. There are designated places (or seats). There are specific norms on the part of hosts to receive guests. Guests are also expected to behave in a particular way. In this context, the predicted behaviour is a pretty straight forward matter.

Similar is the case with a planned business meeting. The seating arrangement, the agenda, and the provision of presiding over the meeting clearly signal a specific behavioural expectations. The variability of behaviour is severely reduced. Most of the people behave as per prevailing norms. Any one in this situation can foretell what would be the behaviour of the other persons.

Of course, there may be some exception to this rule. A small number of people may behave in unusual manner. Yet, the clarity and structure of the situation would seriously limit the individual variation.

As a contradistinction, personality becomes a powerful determinant when conditions are ambiguous. In the midnight, a bus may come to an abrupt halt. The situation is fairly unstructured. Many passengers are asleep or in a dozing state. If it stops suddenly, different people may react to the situation differently. Some people may howl, some may cling to their seats. Some people may get out of the bus to inquire what has happened. Some people may surround the driver. When the situation is hazy, people react in distinctive ways that characterize their personality characteristics.

A basic learning point from this analysis suggests a dynamic approach. It is not wise to trivialize personality factors. It is also not prudent to consider personality as an all-pervasive explanatory concept. Depending on the clarity of situation, the significance of personality factors gains or loses.

If you are a clever person and you have the task of making a prediction as to how a person would behave, just assess the clarity of the situation. If the situation is pretty clear, offer the driver's seat to Mr. Situation and expect that normative behaviours would follow.

The Unconscious: The Hidden Mind

The working mind is mostly revealed through our conscious experiences. However, many people believe there is a hidden mind that Sigmund Freud called the *unconscious*. There are many situations where we plan and act. There are explicit reasons behind such actions. But there are cases where causes of behaviour are not available. In these cases, causes are thought to lie in a mental territory called *the unconscious*.

It was not Freud who first used the term. In fact several others gave indication about an inaccessible territory of mind. Yet, it was Freud who provided details of the unconscious and delineated its attributes.

In the beginning, Freud was a neurologist and a physician. In course of his work as a physician, he offered therapeutic suggestions to patients including mental patients. He found that the therapeutic interventions did not produce lasting results. Patients returned to him for further advice. This offered him an insight that cure would be possible only when inner conflicts are eliminated from the psyche.

Freud had a second insight from a different source. As a medical practioner he had opportunity to come across hypnosis as a treatment method. In typical hypnosis methods, hypnotized patients are given the suggestions. Although cases of hypnosis produced positive outcomes for the time being, it did not offer permanent cure. On the contrary, Freud observed that another practice called *hypnocatharsis* produced good results. In hypocatharsis, hypnotized patients were advised not to forget symptoms, but to recall and express conflicts that were bothering. This observation led Freud to believe that release of pent-up emotion is more useful and repression is harmful.

Drawing on those two insights, Freud conceptualized the psyche as a energy system where energy can not be created nor destroyed. However, one form of energy can be transformed to a different modality.

Freud constructed a topography of mind. According to him mind consists of three layers: Conscious, subconscious and the unconscious. At any point of time, we are aware of certain events and experiences. This constitutes the conscious mind. As you are reading this article, you are aware of your present behaviour and its cause. The thin layer that divides the conscious and the unconscious is the subconscious preconscious mind. Suppose you have given appointment to your friend asking him/her to meet you at this place. Although you are not constantly remembering this while you are reading, there is every possibility that you would be aware next moment. This is in your subconscious (preconscious).

The unconscious mind is the store-house of repressed (suppressed) materials. It contains unfulfilled wishes, immoral thoughts, sexual impulses, fears, anxiety and many other forbidden thoughts. Accordingly, to Freud, the unconscious constitutes a major portion of our mind

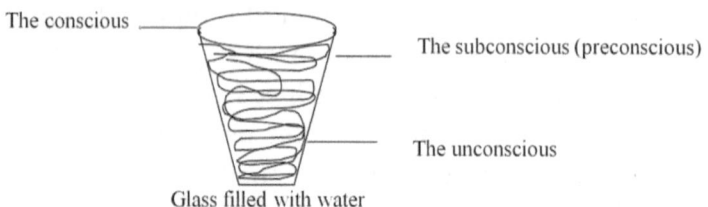
Glass filled with water

(psyche). Just as a tip of the Ice-berg floating in the water is visible, so also only a small portion of mind is conscious mind.

The unconscious is alogical in the sense opposites can stand for same thing. The unconscious has no regard for time. Events of different period may coexist. It also disregards space. The size and distance relationship are distorted.

The most important attribute of the unconscious is its motivational nature. According to Freud, most of the psychic energy is directed to repressing the tabooed material into the unconscious and finding indirect ways of expressing the unconscious items (when censorship is low). Since the unconscious is basically store of the tabooed materials, the mode of expression is in the form of disguise such as dreams, slip of tongue, everyday error, and neurotic and psychotic symptoms.

Dream: The Royal Road to the Unconscious

Dream is a common experience with an uncommon complexity. Many experts of different persuasions have attempted to explain why we dream the way dream. Yet, none has achieved success comparable to Freud's accomplishment. In fact, his book *Interpretation of Dreams* (published in 1900) is considered Freud's magnum opus.

The interpretation of dream is based on Freud's construct of the unconscious. As pointed out earlier, the unconscious is a store house of forbidden thoughts. It contains repressed aggression, suppressed sexual impulses, immoral thoughts, fears, anxiety and so on. These repressed materials constantly seek expression in some form. But the conscious mind functions as a censor and does not allow free and uninhibited express. Accordingly, such a denial of expression forces the unconscious to adopt a disguised form. Of all the disguised forms of expressions, dream is a royal road. The unconscious reveals itself through dream.

Although dream is a convenient avenue for expression of unconscious materials, the dream has the additional function of protecting the sleep. Accordingly, the real thought contents (*latent contents*) are transformed into disguised contents *(manifest contents)*. This transformation subserves two functions. First, it gives vent to unfulfilled wishes by expressing the unconscious. Second, it protects sleep as the person does not get up owing to the disguised nature of the original thought contents.

In other words, each dream has some manifest contents (the visuals we see) and latent contents (the real meaning). The task of a dream analyst is to convert the manifest contents into latent contents. It is obvious that dream has a lot of symbolism. On the basis of the analysis of patients' history, cultural milieu and other evidence, Freudians evolved a list of symbols. For example, a boat in a dream symbolizes woman's body whereas a snake symbolizes, a male sex organ.

Freud has identified four mechanisms of dream interpretation. These include *displacement, dramatization, secondary elaboration* and *condensation.*

In displacement, the focus is shifted to another object or person which is less threatening. Suppose a boy is attending to his father who has been sick for a long time. The body is extremely stressed and tired. All on a sudden, an inappropriate thought may cross his mind. "It's better if my father dies". The thought comes and goes. However, the boy is now guilt-ridden that he is very ungrateful to his loving father. As soon as he realizes his mistake, the thought is forced into his unconscious. But he would be awakened if he dreams the death of his father. It is very likely that the boy dreams the death of his teacher or his employer or any other leader symbolizing father figure. The focus is shifted from father to another significant person.

In dramatization, a single forbidden thought is elaborated in the form of narratives. The form of narrative is so dramatic that the dreamer is unable to recognize the original thought. For example, a poor girl may see a gorgeously dressed lady with beautiful ornaments. She may wish for a moment to own the valuable dress and ornaments. But she represses the ideas soon after she realizes that this is not possible. In her dream she may see a lot of events such as a marriage ceremony. Just for a second she may see herself holding an umbrella with gold embroidery. This is an illustration of dramatization.

The condensation mechanism is one where an elaborate forbidden thought is condensed into a momentary dream visualization. The person might have thought for hours. Yet, in the dream the disguised contents last for a few minutes or some seconds.

Finally, the mechanism of secondary elaboration is interesting. In this case, the central part of the thought comes in the dream for a few minutes or some seconds. But unrelated and secondary thought contents are elaborated in the dream. For example, an individual may wish to hurt an important person. But he represses it in view of the threat of punishment. In this case, person may dream many things relating to the house, movement and activities of the target person. In the midst of such elaboration, a flash of bumping into the target person may appear as a manifest content. Since the main thought is camouflaged by these elaboration, the dreamer is not aware of the forbidden intention as it appears.

As discussed, psychoanalysts attempt to convert manifest contents into latent contents so that the true story underlying the dream could be revealed. While doing so, they keep track of the mechanisms discussed earlier and the possible symbols manifest in the dream. Of course, a professional analyst attempts to derive a true picture of the client. In this process, the analyst cross-validates the findings of the dream with other sources. In other words, the findings obtained from the dream analysis must fit with conclusions derived from other sources such as analysis of important life events, test results and free association (target person talking out freely about his/her problems). If information obtained from all these sources are congruent, the information is accepted. If not, findings obtained from the interpretation of dream is not taken seriously.

Finally, it is important to point out that a number of post-Freudians suggested some revision in dream interpretation. More specifically, Jung explained dream as a manifestation of *Collective unconscious* (not individual consciousness as postulated by Freud). According to Jung, human behaviour is influenced by racial experiences-experiences accumulated over centuries through transmission across generations. This collective experience constitutes collective consciousness and cultural archetypes. A person, according to Jung, dreams a snake not because of his/her repressed sexual impulses as postulated by Freud, but he/she dreams it because it is a product of collective conscious. The snake is worshipped in many cultures as a symbol of masculinity. Thus, Jung shifted the emphasis from individual unconscious to collective unconscious. In other words, dream contents are reflections, not of individual experiences, but of collective experiences.

The Horses that Draw the Cart of Personality

While the theory of the unconscious represents geoghy of mind, Freud's view of the structural components of personality denotes the historical evolution of mind during one's growth period. According to Sigmund Freud, personality is an undifferentiated structure in the beginning. The infant in the beginning is a bundle of biological instincts. Freud calls it *id* component of the personality. Its primary source is biological energy and it is governed by pleasure principle. It attempts to do anything that affords pleasure. It does not care for life that does not afford pleasure. The other feature of *id* is its unconscious nature. The *id* remains submerged entirely in the unconscious.

Gradually the infant begins interaction with the environment. But interaction with the environment brings a new set of experiences. The infant learns that everything does not afford pleasure. The infant that used to derive pleasure out of sucking mother's breast attempts to put a candle into its mouth, but gets hurt. The infant learns that some objects cause pain while others cause pleasure. This new form of experience prompts him or her not to care for objects that endanger life. Thus, a new structure crystallizes out. Freud calls it ego. The ego is a product of interaction with the realities of environment. It is governed by reality principle. The ego stays in the realm of the conscious.

Subsequently the infant is subjected to forces of socialization. Parents and other adults teach him/her the notions of wrong and right. They use a lot of do's and don'ts. The socialization process leads to the development of another component called *superego*. In our everyday language, superego is nothing but the conscience. Needless to say, superego is governed by moral principle. Most of the contents of superego are stored in memory. Stated differently, most parts of superego are in the preconscious whereas a small part of it in the conscious and a small part of it in the unconscious.

According to Freud, id, ego and superego work in a harmonious way in a balanced personality. Freud compares human personality with a cart driven by three different horses. If horses of id, ego, and superego draw the cart of personality in a coordinated manner, things go well. The individual displays integrated personality. In contrast, personality shows maladaptation if id, ego, and superego do not function in a harmonious manner.

An example would clearly illustrate this point. Suppose a person finds an excessive amount of delicious food. Initially the id impulses would prompt him/her to start eating. But the ego would sound a signal that he/she is an invitee and must wait for the host's request to start eating. Further, the person continues eating and at some point, the superego (conscience) offers a warning—"too much eating is injurious to health". Thus, the checks and balances offered by these three structural components make things easier for an individual. Despite such balance worked out by the coordinated functions of id, ego and superego, some individuals are id-dominated whereas other persons are ego-dominated. Some people are superego-dominated as well. Needless to say, the dominance of one component over other components create an imbalance. Maladjustment can be avoidance if these three components function harmoniously.

Structure of personality

Personality Component	Energy source	Governing Principle
Id	Biological (Instinctual)	Pleasure Principle
Ego	Environmental	Reality Principle
Superego	Socialization	Morality Principle

The Collective Unconscious

The notion of unconscious as proposed by Sigmund Freud was a force to reckon with. It stimulated both thinking and rethinking on the matter. Many people found it to be convenient explanatory concept to account for a number of behaviours which were difficult to grasp otherwise. The cases of everyday psychological errors such as slip of tongue and slip of pen were among such phenomena.

However, the idea of infantile sexuality as the core concept underlying the unconscious was strongly criticized by Freud's closest associates: Adler and Jung. Adler deviated from Freud in an important way. Adler was working with physically handicapped children. He came across an interesting observation. He found that children experiencing difficulty with respect to one sense modality excel in other area. A child having difficulty of vision excels in auditory perception.

This observation led Adler to believe that people, because of some reason or the other, experience inferiority. A possible reason may involve environmental constraint. Because of this perception of environmental constraint, they experience *inferiority*. The feelings of inferiority, in turn, induces a strong motivation for superiority. In other words, striving for superiority shapes human goals and activity.

More specifically, Adler underlines the role of special interest and goal of the individual. Adler thus arrived at a rationally holistic view of human nature whereby all behaviour falls into place in the wake of its goal as water takes a predictable form in the wake of a ship. Any fragment of behaviour could be interpreted by insight into the specific goal of the individual (his/her path to superiority) and could be changed automatically by persuading the person to change his/her goal. Thus, Adler did not presume suppression and repression of conscious thought contents as there were no signs of guilt feelings on the part of individuals.

While Adler was critical of the primitive (biological) force as a determinant of human behaviour, Jung resisted the idea of individual basis of human behaviour. Her attached importance to racial experience and asserted that the *Collective unconscious*, not the individual unconscious is the primary determinant of human behaviour the collective unconscious results out of accumulating experiences across generations. Jung's exposition is very graphic.

This psychic life is the mind of our ancient ancestors, the way in which they thought and felt, the way in which they conceived of life and the world, of gods and human beings. The existence of these historical layers is presumably the source of the belief in reincarnation and in memories of past lives. As the body is a sort of museum of its phylogenetic history, so is the mind. There is no reason for believing that the psyche, with its peculiar structure, is the only thing in the world that has no history beyond is individual manifestation. Even the conscious mind cannot be denied a history extending over at least five thousand years. It is only individual ego-consciousness that has forever a new beginning and an early end. But the unconscious psyche is not only immensely old, it is also able to grow increasingly into an equally remote future. It forms, and is part of, the human species just as much as the body, which is also individually ephemeral, yet collectively of immeasurable duration.

The collective unconscious is the all-controlling deposit of ancestral experience from untold millions of years, the echo of prehistoric world events to which every century adds an infinitesimally small amounts of variation.

The experiences accumulated over several thousands of generations is stored in the form of collective unconscious. The collective unconscious when reflected in the form of dream contents or other forms of thought and behaviour are called *archetypes*. Thus, archetypes are the product of racial experiences. Mother, for example, is an archetype. Similarly, all individuals have maleness and femaleness within themselves. Jung called animesh and anima.

In Jung's terms, dream contents are not necessarily sexual in nature. If a person dreamt a snake, Freud interpreted it as a symbol of male sex organ. However, Jung argued that the dream of a snake is not a reflection of personal unconscious. Snake is worshipped in many cultures as a symbol of masculinity. Consequently, the dream of a snake symbolizes the person's respect for masculinity. A particular dream content is a product of racial experiences, though the features of a specific sociocultural milieu are likely to modify it. The dream of a *'rishi'* is a distinct possibility for an Indian, not for a westerner. On the contrary, the dream of a distant star is a likely occurrence for any one in this world. It signifies a goal in life. This has universal meaning. Thus, collective unconscious is indicative of both universal features and culture specific elements.

The Power of Subliminal Messages

The idea of the unconscious essentially posits a view that we may not be aware of certain thoughts at a given point of time. Whether or not the unconscious materials are sexual in nature may be topic of debate. Sigmund Freud viewed it as essentially irrational and sexual in contents whereas other non-libido theorists do not agree with him. They contend that the materials could be non-sexual as well.

Even if we are not aware of certain materials, these are likely to influence the way we feel, think and act. A modern form of demonstrating this proposition involves the use of subliminal message.

Limen means threshold. For conscious experiences, a stimulate must reach a particular boundary level. For example, we can hear a sound when only it crosses a particular intensity. Similarly, we can read an item (say a number or a word) when it is exposed for specific period of time. But what happen if it is exposed for a smaller proportion of time. We can barely see it. This level is called subliminal level.

One would be curious to know whether an advertisement presenting subliminal message (say, buy popcorn) would induce buying behaviour for that advertised product. There is some evidence to suggest that such "hidden messages" work. In other words, very very low pitch of voice advocating a way of behaviour may produce advocated behaviour. The message could be used to help people to keep well or to build confidence.

However, it would be over-generalized to claim that it would influence all sorts of behaviour. In the past, there was a well-publicized law suit against the music leader of Rock Group in the United States. The parents alleged that their sons committed suicide because of the subliminal message "do it" hidden in their music. Eventually parents lost their case against the group.

Of course, the magnitude of influences is controversial. Yet, the experimental demonstration of the power of subliminal message proves a point in favour of Freudian claim. It suggests that certain thoughts of which individuals are not aware can affect what a person think, feel and does.

Psychologists generally agree that subliminal perception exists, but they differ about how powerful and widespread the effect is. There is no strong evidence of its power in advertising, nor any evidence of the therapeutic value of subliminal tapes (with hidden message telling you to relax).

There has been experimental support in favour of subtle effect of subliminal messages. In a study, children were exposed to a subliminal message- "Mother loves me". It was presented for some milliseconds; as a results, no child could read it. This was the case of subliminal perception. A similar group of children were exposed to another subliminal message- "Mother leaves me".

Following the exposure to subliminal messages, both groups of children were tested for their memory for some words which were normally presented. The free-recall test indicated that the second group performed poorer than the first group. It was postulated that the second group was experiencing anxiety because of the negative subliminal message ("Mother leaves me"). Otherwise, there is no reason as to why the groups would differ. Thus, the effect of subliminal message is accepted, though the extent of effect is debated.

A Tale of Three Personality Types

Psychologists are not the sole contributors to the growth of psychological knowledge. There are occasions when people beyond the territory of professional psychology have significantly enriched our knowledge of human behaviour. In recent decades, one such major break-through has been achieved by cardiac surgeons.

The cardiac surgeons- Friedman and Rosenman- were wedded to work in San Francisco hospital. In course of their treatment of heart patients, they came across an interesting observation. They found that people with cardiac problem exhibited specific personality characteristics. In stead of using any psychological jargon, they termed it Type A Personality. Of course, subsequently they changed the terminology and called it *Type A Behavioural Pattern*.

People with "Type A Behaviour Pattern" are vulnerable to heart problems. They have three distinctive personality characteristics. First, they exhibit a great deal of *time urgency*. They feel upset if things are not done in time. They feel unhappy if deadlines are not met. Second, they display *achievement strivings*. They keep-up doing hard work to accomplish something significant in life. Third, they have *moderate degree of aggressiveness.* This does not imply that they tend to do harm to others. Rather they are assertive and stand up for their own perception, beliefs and values.

In other words, these people can be described as "rush-rush" personalities-the kind of personalities we find in modern multinational companies. Apart from these three distinctive features, there is fastness in other forms of their activities. They eat fast, walk fast, talk fast and respond fast. As indicated earlier, people with these behaviour patterns are more susceptible to coronary diseases compared to individuals with Type B behaviour patterns.

People with Type B behaviour patterns can be deserted as "go-slow" types. They are very casual about many things. They are not eager to achieve. Their assertion level is low.

The distinction between these two types of personalities may lead to an erroneous conclusion. Although the specialists are indicating a linkage between Type A behaviour pattern and cardio vascular diseases, they are not suggesting the relinquishment of Type A behaviour pattern. The scientists argue that Type A behaviour pattern is otherwise indicative of productive behaviour. These people contribute significantly towards the productivity in their families, organizations and societies. Hence Type A behaviour is not to be discarded.

The scientists advise that people will Type A behaviour patterns need to engage themselves in stress-reducing activities. Activities such as relaxation, exercise, yoga and meditation need to constitute an essential aspect of their daily lives. If they take up such stress-reducing strategies, they would be able to experience enrichment of their lives.

Although not equally supported, two clinical psychologists have identified what they call cancer personality-Personality C. Type C is the name given to constellation of characteristics including the tendencies to deny and express emotions to avoid conflict and to be overly agreeable. The researchers observed that people who had cancer were more likely than those without cancer were (1) more unable to express hostile emotions, (2) had more unresolved tension concerning a parental figure, and (3) had more sexual disturbances. However, it was not clear whether these characteristics induced some probability of cancer susceptibility or these characteristics were the result following cancer diagnosis.

Are you interested to determine your type A or type B profile
To determine your profile encircle the number on the continuum (verbal descriptions represent end points) that best represents your behaviour on that dimension.
Am casual about appointment 1 2 3 4 5 6 7 8 Am never late Am not competitive 1 2 3 4 5 6 7 8 Am very competitive Never feel rushed even under pressure 1 2 3 4 5 6 7 8 Always feel rushed Take things one at a time 1 2 3 4 5 6 7 8 Try to do many things at a time. Do things slowly 1 2 3 4 5 6 7 8 Do things fast (talking, walking, etc) Express feelings 1 2 3 4 5 6 7 8 "sit" on feelings Have many interests 1 2 3 4 5 6 7 8 Have many interests outside work

Total your score
Multiply it by 5
The interpretation of your score is as follows:

Number of points	Type of personality
Less than 90	B
90 to 99	B⁺
100 to 105	A⁻
106 to 119	A
120 or more	A⁺

Stress-awareness

Stress can be defined simply the response of body to any demand made on it. More accurately speaking, stress is experienced when *demands* exceed *resources*. In the beginning, ideas about different categories of demands and resources are needed. The box presents three types of demands and resources.

Types of demands and resources

Types	Demands	Resources
1. Physical	Lack of oxygen, excessive heat, excessive coolness	Money, materials, physical health, other assets
2. Personal	Examination, job interview, important assignments	Ability, skills, self-confidence
3. Social	Social obligation, taking care of the sick, taking care of the young	Support from family, friends, and colleagues

As indicated above, demands and resources are placed on two side of the mental balance. If resources weigh more, stress is averted. If demands exceed, stress is experienced. Of course, any amount of stimulation does not cause problem. Infact Greeks use an expression "eustress" where the prefix "eu" stands for "pleasant". In other words, some amount of stimulation is quite comfortable. What we call stress is really distress or overstimulation.

In stress-literature, two interesting terms are used: Russ (Rust-out Stress Syndrome) and Buss (Burn-out Stress Syndrome). It implies that there is optimal level (ideal) of stimulation. There is distress below this level (RUSS); there is also discomfort beyond this level (BUSS).

There are *physical* warning signs of stress. These include: tiredness, sleeplessness, increased pulse or heart rate, rapid or shallow breathing, tenseness of muscles, perspiration, and tightening of stomach.

Similarly, there are some psychological warning signs. These include irritability, procrastination, sadness, worry, racing thoughts, brooding, and forgetfulness.

There are also some symptoms that are designated psychophysiological (psychosomatic). These symptoms start as psychological difficulties but end up as physical disorders. These include disorders of asthma, peptic ulcer and hyper tension. It would be quite interesting to know something about their origin.

Every one knows that human body is equipped with an autonomic nervous system. During normal period, our central nervous system regulates our activities. However, autonomic nervous system becomes active during emergency period. At the time of emergency (emotional state), central nervous system loses its grip over the body and regular functions such as digestion are suspended for a while. On the contrary, the autonomic nervous system triggers some hormones that help the organism to meet emergency functions. Regular activity being suspended, more energy and blood are available for other organs. For example, the organism gets more energy is run, to lift objects, etc.

If stress experience is occasional and infrequent, no permanent damage occurs. A parallelism may be drawn between an animal and an individual. Suppose a deer sees a tiger, gets frightened, and runs for life. As soon as the deer sees that the tiger is out of sight, it gradually gets back to normalcy. The activity of autonomic nervous system stops and central nervous system brings. But things are not so simple for human beings. The thought of fear persists even if the object of fear is out of sight. Thus, prolonged and frequent activation of the autonomic nervous system cause damage to human organs.

The prolonged stress experience induces psychophysiological disorder such as asthma, peptic ulcer and hyper-tension. However, one may be curious to know why some people are affected by asthma while others get hypertension. There are two possible explanations. Medical scientists believe that the organ which is inherently weak gets affected. If a person's respiratory system has some problem in the beginning, the stress would cause asthma. If inherent weakness is associated with circulatory system, the individual would be a victim of hyper tension.

According to psychologists, the problem originates depending on the personality types. If individuals are aggressive, they are likely to get into the trap of hypertension. If individuals are markedly anxious, they are vulnerable to peptic ulcer. If people are over-dependent, they are susceptible to asthmatic disorder.

Where Do Stressors Come From?

Everyone desires a stress-free life. Unfortunately, stressors attack us as thugs and snatch our pockets of happiness. In order to combat stress, it is essential to know their genesis. As suggested by the following diagram, stress could originate from any of these spheres.

Broad Environment

- Self
- Family
- Work
- Immediate environment

The Individual himself or herself may a source of stress, even if other members are isolated. The internal conflict of beliefs, attitudes, values, goals and personal attributes may be a source of stress. For example, the individual may believe in something, but does something contradictory. Literature is replete with this kind of internal conflicts (stress).

Similarly, stressors may spring from family, work place, immediate environment (neighbourhood) and broader environment (region, state, country, continent, world). A meaningful way of locating stressors would involve a three-fold classification of stressors: cataclysmic, everyday life event stressors and micro-stressors.

Cataclysmic stressors. These are also known as catastrophes. A disaster that affects a larger section of population belongs to this category. The earth-quake, floods, hurricane, tornados, cyclone, drought, and volcanic eruption are examples of these cataclysmic stressors. Similarly, threat of foreign aggression, fear of epidemic, and fear of nuclear explosion are also stressors. There are many surveys that have indicated increased suicide rate following these cataclysmic stressors.

Life Event Stressors. A major source of stressors happens to be the negative life event such as death of spouse or loved ones, loss of job, accident, financial loss, sickness in the family, and so on. Even some positive events such as marriage generate some amount of instability, as it takes time to get adjusted to a new system of life. In fact many psychologists and counsellors measure the amount of stress an individual is experiencing by asking him/her to indicate the amount of imbalance he/she feels with respect to each of a list of life events.

Sample items from the social readjustment rating scale

The events listed can be used to estimate the amount of recent stress in your life (you'll notice that this scale omits many events common among college students–such as graduation and relationships with friends). Read each item indicate the amount of imbalance you feel with respect to each of the possible event by writing a number from 0 to 100. Note that you can use a base line reference. As shown for death of spouse and marriage.

Life Event			
1. Death of spouse	100	16. Son or daughter leaving home	
2. Divorce		17. Outstanding personal achievement	
3. Jail term or imprisonment		18. Major change in work hours or conditions	
4. Death of a close family member		19. Move to a new residence	
5. Major personal injury or illness		20. Transfer to a new place	
6. Marriage	50	21. Taking out a loan (e.g., for a new car)	
7. Losing one's job		22. Change in sleeping habits	
8. Pregnancy		23. Change in eating habits	
9. Sexual difficulties		24. Vacation	
10. Addition of a new family member		25. Minor law violations (traffic fine, etc.)	
11. Change in financial state			
12. Death of a close friend			
13. Change to a different line of work			
14. A large mortgage			
15. Change in status at work			

Interpretation
Sum your ratings across all 25 items and divide it by 25. Interpret as follows.

Less than 20: Quite normal, not to be worried
21-30: Stress signal-be watchful
31-40: Marked stress-Take steps
41-50: High stress-Consult experts
Above 50: Very high stress-follow stress-reducing measures and consult experts.

Micro-Stressors. Micro stressors are molecular in their size, yet the continuous and repeated encounter with these stimuli cause damage. Everyday exposure to traffic gum, exposure to high intensity traffic sound, unavailability of cooking gas, power interruption, and similar such events constitute micro-stressors. A micro-stressor may not be harmful if it is occasional. But its repetition brings problem.

It has been shown the people who live near to airport indicate higher blood pressure because of constant exposure to high intensity sound. Even new-born babies show such tendency in the direction of heightened pressure.

You Cope Well When You Confront

Stress is inevitable. No one can prevent it. But people can try to minimize its harmful effects on health. There are numerous ways to cope (see Table). There are two general types: problem-focused coping and emotion-focused coping. In *Problem-focused coping,* people use cognitive and behavioural efforts to reduce stress by overcoming the source of the problem. While encountering difficulties in schools, students can study harder, discuss the problem with teachers, and can reduce their workloads. Faced with interpersonal problems, people can talk it out. In work place, individuals can consult with their boss or seek a new job.

A second approach is *emotion-focused coping.* It consists of various efforts to manage our emotional reaction to a stressful situation rather than trying to change it. If you are struggling at school, at work, or in a relationship, you can keep a stiff upper lip, accept what is happening, tune out, or vent your emotion. Research has shown that people tend to take an active, problem-focused approach when they think they can overcome a stressor. They fall back on an emotion-focused approach when they perceive the problem to be out their control.

Problem-focused coping seems like the prime candidate for a starring role in the war against stress. Surely our most active direct and assertive efforts are associated with better mental health. We benefit from confronting a stressor head-on rather than avoiding it. We are guilty of procrastination and purposive delay in the beginning or completing a task, which is often accompanied by feeling of discomfort.

In many cases, people generally tend to procrastinate. Students who anticipate discomforting grades tend to put off their preparation and presentation. They gain some short-term benefits by avoiding the situation. Later in the examination, procrastinators are under great stress and report having symptoms of illness. The short-term benefits are overweighed by the long-term costs.

In dealing with challenges it is **better to confront and control than to avoid.** Of course, there are some precautions. First, to exert control, a person must stay vigilant, alert, and actively engaged which is physiologically taxing. Second, control brings with it the burden of responsibility. It may induce the fear that the effort may fail.

When we use the word *control*, we usually have in mind active efforts to manage something. But control comes in many forms. Knowledge is a form of control. Knowing why something is happening increases our chance of making sure it goes our way-if not now, then the next time. Sometimes, we can even cope effectively with tragedies.

Ways of Coping with stress

These statements describe some coping strategies that people say they use. The strategies are listed in order from those that are relatively common to those that are less common.

Planning/Active Coping • I try to come up with a strategy about what to do. • I take additional action to try to get rid of the problem.	**Suppression of Competing Activities** • I put aside other activities to concentrates on this. • ….. If necessary let other this slide a little.
Positive Reinterpretation • I look for something good in what is happening. • I try to make it seem more positive.	**Mental Disengagement** • I turn to work… to take my mind off things. • I go to the movies or watch TV, to think about it less.
Acceptance • I learn to live with it. • I accept that this has happened and can't be changed.	**Turning to Religion** • I seek God's help. • I try to find comfort in my religion.
Seeking Social Support • I talk to someone about how I feel. • I ask people who had similar experiences what they did.	**Behavioural Disengagement** • I give up the attempt to get what I want. • I admit to myself that I can't deal with it.
Restraint Coping • I force myself to wait for the right time to do something. • I make sure not to make matters worse by acting too soon.	**Denial** • I refuse to believe that it has happened. • I pretend that it hasn't really happened.
Focussing on/Venting Emotions • I get upset and let my emotions out. • I let my feelings out.	**Alcohol and Drugs** • I drink alcohol or take drugs to think about it less.

When Emotion-Focused Coping is Inevitable

There are many instances of emotion-focused coping. These include acceptance, denial, a focusing on or venting of emotions, mental and behavioural disengagements, or turning to religion. There are two general ways to deal with the emotional aspects of stress: Shutting down and opening up.

In many cases, we react to stress by shutting down and trapping to deny or suppress the unpleasant thoughts and feelings. A severe trauma with long-lasting consequences-such as the death of a loved one-can cause us to question some of our most basic and cherished assumptions about the meaningfulness of life. People who are confronted with serious threats to their worldviews often need psychological breathing space. If unable to avoid or deny these threats early in the coping process, they may become overwhelmed.

An adaptive form of avoidance is distraction. When terrorists take innocent victims hostage, an effective way of coping with this frightening situation involves *distraction*. In this kind of situation, where individuals have little actual control over events, distraction and other emotion-focused coping is more effective than problem-focused coping of exerting control.

In distraction, people generally tend to suppress the unwanted thoughts. Although potentially effective, the suppression can also have a paradoxical effect. When people try not to think of a terrorist attack, they may fail to keep the image from popping to mind. Sometimes, it is harder to try not to think about something. A possible solution to this rebound effect is to use focused distraction. Individuals may be successful in deeply thinking about a substitute image that would dispel the rebound image. In Indian tradition, people can easily think of their *ista-devata* to replace the disturbing image.

Further research suggests that just as shutting down, at times, can have benefits, so too can the opposite form of coping: opening up. Psychotherapies, self-help groups, and various religious rituals all have something in common. They offer a chance for people to confide in someone.

The healing power of opening up has been experimentally demonstrated. A researcher brought college students to a laboratory and asked them to talk into a tape recorder or write for twenty minutes either about past traumas or about trivial daily events. While speaking or writing, the students were physiologically aroused and upset. Many tearfully recounted accidents, failures, loneliness and shattered relationship. When they opened up, their systolic blood pressure levels rose during the disclosures. But pressure, dipped below their pre-experiment levels. The students even exhibited a decline in their number of visits to the doctor over the next six months. Other studies have shown that keeping personal secrets can be stressful and that "letting it out" and "getting it off our chest" can have therapeutic effects on mental and physical health. It appears that confession may be good for the body as well as the mind.

Longtime back Freud stressed the value of *catharsis* (a discharge of tension) like taking the lid off a boiling pot of water to slow the boiling. Further-more, talking about a problem can help us to sort out our thoughts, understand the problem better, and gain insights. Whatever may be the reason, opening up can be therapeutic provided the listener is trusted.

Proactive Coping

Coping can be, seen as an ongoing process by which we try to prevent as well as coping consists of up-front effort to word off or modify the onset of a stressful event. The first line of defence in this regard consists of the accumulation of resources–persons, financial, social, and otherwise–that can later, if needed, serve as a buffer against stress.

People can occupy many different roles in life-friend, teacher, cricket player, and so on. It has been shown that people having many distinct roles are less prone to stress-related illness. These are exceptions of course. People with many negative identities do have problems. But having *many positive identities* is very helpful.

In some quarters, it is believed that self-complexity (performance of multiple roles)is a stressor. These people cite the case of dual career woman. They argue that multiple role of a woman as a job-holder and home maker is a constant source of stress. Yet, research documents that employed women who have positive attitude towards job indicate greater wellness than unemployed women. Similarly, employed men who value family involvement experience less stress than persons having no family obligation. Thus, the quality of experience associated with multiple roles brings the difference.

The accumulation of social resources works well as a preventive strategy. Family members' friends, loved ones, faith community members and colleagues constitute a network system that buffers stress. Quite sometime ago, a researcher was very prudent in bringing together a number of breast cancer patients. The arrangement was made so that they could cry, laugh, and talk together. Regular meetings of the group were arranged. As expected, the mental health of these women was better than a comparable group of women who did not have such opportunity.

In addition to this expected results, there was another interesting findings. These women lived longer compared to their counter parts having no such benefits. The support system provides help to mitigate stress. The collaborative discussion of problems, generation of solution alternatives and emotional catharsis prove to be beneficial. It has been shown that people with lots of friends have easy time. Even people with pets report less stress than lonely people.

Apart from the number of friends and supporters, the quality of experience is also important. A person having a small number of intimate or close friends is likely to be better-off than an individual with many so-called friends. The intensity of intimacy at least with a few close associates is instrumental in providing appropriate emotional release and channelization.

Finally, it is important to recognize that the availability of support is a crucial factor. The individual must be convinced that he or she can always find someone if he/she needs at a juncture. This belief strengthens the coping resources of the individual.

Points to recapitulate
- Develop multiple positive roles to buffer stress.
- Accumulate resources, build a strong and extended social network.
- Establish intimate relationship with a few close persons.
- Make sure that support is available at the time of need.

Attention Deficit Trait (ADT)

Ravi is a top executive in a multinational corporate office. He is intelligent and smart. He has been a remarkably overachiever. Yet, his present performance is surprising many. He is robbed of his flexibility and his sense of humour. His ability to deal with the unknown has gone down. He himself is surprised at his under performance. What has really happened to Ravi?

Ravi is not being only one affected by the modern epidemic called attention deficit trait. It adversely affecting a large number of executives. Caused by brain overload, attention deficit trait (ADT) is now rampant in large organization. The core symptoms are distractibility, inner frenzy, and impatience priorities, and managing time. These symptoms can undermine the work of an otherwise gifted executive.

Those with ADT usually possess rare talents and gifts. These gifts often go unnoticed and undeveloped because of the problems caused by the condition's negative symptoms. The negative symptoms include a tendency to procrastinate and miss deadlines. Such people struggle with disorganization and tardiness. They can be forgetful and drift away mentally in the middle of a conversation or while reading. Their performance can be inconsistent, brilliant one moment and unsatisfactory the next. ADT sufferers also tend demonstrate impatience and lose focus, oddly enough they are under stress handling multiple inputs. This is chemically similar to the medication doctors use to treat ADT. Finally, people with ADT sometimes self- medicate with excessive alcohol or other substances. Found children in the form hyperactivity, has a neurological base. Unlike ADD, a neurological disorder that has a genetic component, and can be aggravated by environment and physical factors, ADT springs entirely from the environmental condition. Link the traffic jam, ADT is an artifact of modern life. It is brought on by the demands on our time and attention that have exploded over the past years. The symptoms of ADT come upon a person gradually. The sufferer does not experience a single crisis but a series of mirror emergencies which he or she tries harder and to deal with. Gradually he or she reaches a breaking point.

The role of brain

While brain scans cannot display anatomical difference between people with "normal" brains and people suffering from ADT, studies have shown that as the human brain is asked to process dizzying amount of data, its ability to solve problems declines and the number of mistakes increases.

Blessed with the largest cortex in all of nature owners of this trillion- celled organ today put singular pressure on the frontal and prefrontal lobes (together called frontal lobes). This region governs executive function (EF). EF guides decision making and planning, the organization and prioritization of information and ideas time management, and various other sophisticated, uniquely human, managerial function. As long as our frontal lobes are in charge, every things is fine.

Beneath the frontal lobe lie the parts of the brain devoted to survival. These deep centres govern basic functions like sleep, hunger, sexual desire, breathing, heart rate, as well as crudely, positive and negative emotions. When you are doing well and operating at peak level the deep centres send up messages of satisfaction and joy. They pump up your motivation help you maintain attention and not interfere with working memory. But when you are confronted with a brain jam, your brain may begin to panic.

The most dangerous element is fear. Fear drifts us into survival mode and prevents from learning and understanding. If a real tiger is about to attack your survival is the mode you want to be in. if you are trying to deal with a difficult task, survival mode is highly unpleasant.

When frontal lobes approach capacity and we fear that we can't keep up the relationship between the higher and the lower regions of brain takes an ominous turn. Thousands of years of evolution have conditioned the higher brain not to ignore the demand of the lower brain. In survival mode, the deep centres become central and direct the higher region. As a result, the whole brain gets caught in a neurological trap. The deep regions interpret the messages of overload they receiver from the frontal lobes in the same way they interpret everything primitively. They fore signals of fear, anxiety, impatience irritability, anger or panic. Because survival signals are irresistible, the frontal lobes get stuck.

Meanwhile, in response to what is going on in the brain the rest of the body particularly the endocrine respiratory cardiovascular, musculoskeletal, and peripheral nervous system has shifted into cross mode. In survival mode, the person makes impulsive judgment. He is robbed of his flexibility, his sense of humour, and his ability to deal with the unknown. He forgets the big picture, and the goals and values. He loses his creativity and his ability to change plans. At these moments, he is prone to melting down.

Controlling ADT

Though ADT does not reach such extreme proportions it does wreak havoc among some people. Because no two brains are alike, some people deal with these conditions better than other. While attention deficit disorder (ADD) requires medical the treatment of ADT certainty does not ADT can be controlled only by creatively engineering one's environment and one's emotional and physical health.

Promoting positive emotions. The most important step in controlling ADT is to create an environment in which the brain can function at its best. This means building a positive fear- free emotional atmosphere because emotion is the on/off switch for executive functioning.

There are neurological reasons why ADT occurs less in environments where people are in physical contact and where they trust and respect one another. When you comfortably connect with a colleague, even if you are dealing with an overwhelming problem, the deep centres of the brain send messages through pleasure centres. Thus human connection helps.

In contrast, people who work in isolation are more likely to suffer from ADT. Fostering connections and reducing fear promote brain power. When you make time at least every four to six hours for a "human moment", a face- to – face exchange with a person you like, you are giving your brain what it needs. **Taking physical care of brain.** Sleep, a good diet and exercise are critical for staying off ADT. There is ample documentation to suggest that sleep deprivation generates a host of problems including impaired decision making and reduced creativity. We vary in how much sleep we require. A good rule to thumb is that you are getting enough sleep if you are getting up without an alarm clock.

Diet also plays a crucial role in promoting brain health. Many people habitually take simple carbohydrates containing sugar. This leads to rapid fluctuation in insulin level and the brain, which requires glucose for energy for proper functioning is left either glutted or gaping. This is not optimal for cognitive functioning. The brain does better if the blood sugar level is relatively stable. Hence it is better to take complex carbohydrates found in fruits and vegetables, Protein is important. It is also useful to take a multivitamin everyday as well as supplementary Omega-3 fatty acids, an excellent source of which is fish oil.

Physical exercise induces the body to produce an array of chemical the brain loves. These chemicals promote growth of brain nerves. It is advisable to exercise at least half an hour at least every other day.

Developing healthy habits. It is essential that a person must organize the work habit. First there must be strategies to break down large tasks into small ones. You must keep a section of your work space or desk clean at all times. Similarly, you must keep a portion of the day free appointment, e-mail, and other distraction so that can think and plan.

When you start your day, don't allow yourself to get sucked into worries of e-mail. Attend to a critical task instead. Set aside a limited amount of time for taking care of e- mail. Ask an assistant or a colleague to indicate that the time is up.

It is helpful to pay attention to times of the day when one can do his best. It is better to do the most important work then and save the rote work for other times.

Protecting frontal lobes. In order to stay out of survival mode, it is essential to keep one's lower brain from usurping control take the time you need to comprehend what is going on to learn, to ask questions and digest what has been said.

If you begin to feel overwhelmed, try the mind-clearing tricks. Do an easy and routine task. Reset the calendar on your watch or write a memo on a neutral topic. Write a paragraph on something unrelated to your project. (a description of your house.) Open a dictionary and read meaning of a few words.

ADT is a real threat to all of us. If we do not manage it, it manages us. But an understanding of ADT and application of practical method would greatly improve our ability to handle it properly. Although the challenge is tremendous, our capacity to control and ménage is equally great.

Control your attention deficit trait (ADT)
In General
- Get adequate sleep.
- Watch what you eat. Avoid simple, sugary carbohydrates, Add protein, stick to complex carbohydrates (vegetables, whole grains, fruit).

- Exercise at least 30 minutes every other day.
- Take daily a multivitamin and an omega- 3 fatty acid supplement.

At work

- Do all you can to create a trusting, connected work environment.
- Have a friendly, face-to-face talk with a person you like every four to six hours.
- Break large tasks into smaller ones.
- Keep a section of your work space or desk clear at all times.
- Each day, reserve some "think time" that's free from appointments, e-mail, and phone calls.
- Set aside e-mail until you've completed at least one or two more important tasks.
- Before you leave work each day create a short list of three to five items you will attend to the next day.
- Don't let papers accumulate.
- Pay attention to the times of day when you feel that you are at your best; do your most important work then and save the rote work for other times.
- Do whatever you need to do to work in a more focused way; add background music, walk around, and so, on.
- Ask a friend or an assistant to help you step talking on the telephone, e-mailing, or working too late

When you feel overwhelmed

- Slow down.
- Do an easy rote task: Reset your watch write a note about a neutral topic (such as a description of your

house), read a few dictionary definitions do a short crossword puzzle.

- Move around: Go up and down a flight of stairs or walk briskly.
- Ask for help, delegate a task, or brainstorm with a colleague. In short, do not worry alone

The Heart of Humour

The buffering role of humour in stressful situations is well-admitted in our contemporary life. There are many instances of people returning home after life-disrupting catastrophic events such as floods and cyclones. When these people are interviewed, they relate many incidents that sprinkle humour. It is felt that humour has functioned as a reducer of stress during catastrophic moments.

Comedians have their own understanding of humour. In general, they believe that the secret to creating a successful humour is to mirror the world in a slightly askew way. Like comedians, psychologists are attempting to pin-point exactly what people laugh at and why.

Researchers of humour regard ingenuity as seminal factor in humour. When an idea or an object is our of place, the heart of humour is revealed. Truth plays an important role as well. The Juxtaposition of the two things often gives people a new insight into a familiar situation. In fact, much of the enjoyment of humour may come from seeing familiar situation with new eyes.

Psychologists have long seen that a mismatch between expected and reality leads to humour. In a demonstration study, a psychologist asked people to estimate weights of objects that were either heavier or lighter than looked. Then they were asked to lift these objects and knew their actual weights. It was found that people laughed more when the discrepancy between their estimated weight and actual weight was more. Further, heavier objects brought more laughter than lighter objects.

However, the incongruity brings laughter in a playful atmosphere. Where incongruity poses no threat, it brings no humour. A person walking down the footpath and being hit by a car would bring no humour.

Sometimes humour represents mental gymnastics. The fun of going through mental gymnastics to get to the true meaning of a joke probably accounts for much of our enjoyment of humour. If a joke is to garner more than chuckle, it needs some emotional fire behind it. Some jokes do this by tapping into some unspoken truth. For a long time, a genre of humour has been humour that points to truth that everyone knows but nobody admits. However, for such a joke to be funny the listener has to agree with the related truth. Otherwise, listeners find it offensive.

The utility of humour is well-accepted, of course. It works as a social lubricant. People actually want to connect with others. But they are often anxious. Humour breaks the ice. It reduces anxiety and distracts from the discomfort leading to the formation of friendship bonds.

In a work place, effective managers use humour to ease situations. They use humour to soften unpalatable news. This is also used to get the message across while maintaining good relationship.

There are also occasions where teachers have effectively used humour to implore learning atmosphere.

To be effective, comedy must compliment and not distract from course materials. In fact, instructors who use distracting or inappropriate humour interfere with students' learning.

When used effectively, classroom humour can improve students' performance by reducing anxiety, boosting participation, and increasing students' concentration on the course materials. The benefits are not limited to students; students rate such professors very high.

People may be curious to know whether creation and appreciation of humour is sex-linked. In a study, male and female students were provided with photographs of equally attractive men and women. The person depicted by a photograph was indicated to be an author of a statement. Half of the statements were funny whereas half of the statements were non-funny. Each participant was asked to rate each photograph of the other sex in terms of desirability of relationship. It was found the women participants considered authors of funny statements as more desirable partners compared with authors of non-funny statements. Men participants did not differ. It was implied that although males cite their love for humour they actually prefer appreciating their own humour. Yet, it is strongly agreed that we like people who make us laugh.

Finally, a critical question may be raised with respect to the seat of humour in the brain. Recent evidence suggests that some common neural circuit-probably the brain's reward circuit-the set of structures that underlie the reaction to all sorts of pleasure (from eating to sex) may underlie the response to humour. In addition, when people are exposed to visually involving humours such as cartoons, the brain structures linked with visual processing are activated. Similarly, when people are exposed to verbal and linguistic humours, brain structures linked with sound and language processing are activated. In sum, the involvement of brain structures depends on the type of humour though the reward circuit is involved in all cases.

The Lure of Laughter

How and why people laugh appears to be a question that puzzles many but bothers a few. In general, laughter is not inspired by particularly funny jokes. Instead it is a ubiquitous response to a social situation. People laugh when they are interacting with other people regardless of the jokiness of the conversation, but they don't laugh when they are alone.

Laughter and humour are related, but are different. Laughter is ancient. It is a primate play vocalization. Humour is more modern. There was laughter long before there was humour.

Darwin noticed that chimpanzees and other primates make a panting sound when they are tickled. It is the source from which human laughter evolved.

The very exhaustive analysis of laughter is collected from several sources. It indicates a number of interesting features.

1. Laughter is 30 times more frequent in social situation that in solitary one. When alone, people are much more likely to talk to themselves or smile than to laugh.
2. We often think of laughter as a response to someone

else speaking. But in conversation, speakers are 46 percent more likely to laugh than their audiences.
3. Only 10 to 15 percent of prelaugh comments are even remotely funny.
4. People use laughter as punctuation inserting it more specific places in the vocal stream. (Congenitally deaf people laughed at the same points in signing conversation that hearing people do it in speaking conversation).
5. Laughter is contagious.
6. Sometimes we laugh because we hear a joke. But more often we use laughter for social bonding.

Originally chimp laughter probably arose from the chimps' panting breathing patterns. Over the years, the sound evolved into the signal of humour that it is today. Sometimes we might laugh because we have heard a good social joke, but more often, we use laughter as a tool for social bonding.

Of course, not all laughs are the same. We all recognize a laugh when we hear it, but some are chortles, some chuckles, some guffs, and some snorts. In a 2001 study, a researcher asked college students to rate 50 taped examples of male and female laughter. The examples ranged from "voiced" song-like laughter to "unvoiced" laughter. The researcher found that both male and female listeners responded more positively to the voiced laughter than to the unvoiced laughter. They enjoyed listening to it more and expressed interest in hearing it again.

We use laughter to elicit positive reaction from other people and to communicate to them that we mean them no harm. Humans rely on cooperation with others to an extent that is not seen in other species. But humans are also inherently competitive. So the idea is that we have to evolve some means that let others know that we feel positively towards them. Laughter is that means.

The voiced laughter is a much more reliable indicator of people's positive mood than unvoiced laughter. In other words, a person laughing "hahahia" probably really is happy and nonaggressive. A snorter, though, you just can't be sure about. As a matter of evidence, it is found that autistic children- who tend to produce very honest signals to their internal states-have a much higher ratio of voiced laughter to unvoiced laughter than other children of same age.

Presently neuropsychologists are trying to pinpoint the neuro-anatomical roots of laughter. They are trying to explore whether the parts of the brain involved in laughter are older that those involved in speech.

Bronze Medalists are Happier Than Silver Medalists

People are influenced by how easy it is to imagine events that did not occur. As thoughtful and curious beings, we often are not satisfied to accept what happens to us without wondering, "What if ......?" People's emotional reaction to events are often coloured by *counter factual thinking*. It refers to the tendency to think of alternative outcomes that might have occurred but did not occur. If the imagined result is better than the actual result, we are likely to experience disappointment. If the imagined result is worse, then we react with emotion that range from relief and satisfaction to elation. In interesting ways, the psychological impact of positive and negative events depends on the ways we think about *"what might have been"*.

People don't immerse in counterfactual thinking after every experience. Some situations prompt us. Being on the verge of a better or worse outcome is one such situation. Imagine that you are an Olympic athlete and you have just won a silver medal. Again imagine that you have just own the bronze medal. Which situation would make you feel better? Rationally speaking, you should feel more pride and satisfaction with the silver medal. But what if your achievement has prompted you to engage in counterfactual thinking? What alternative would preoccupy your mind if you had finished in second place? When will be your focus if you had been placed third? Is it possible that the athlete who is better off objectively will feel worse?

To examine this question, one researcher videotaped twenty-one athletes in the 1992. Summer Olympia Games at the moment they realized that they had won a silver or a bronze medal. They were videotaped again during the medal ceremony. The researcher showed these tapes without sound, to people who did not know the order of finish. People were asked to observe these medalists and rate their emotional states on a scale ranging from "agony" to "ecstasy". The interesting result was that bronze medalists, on the averaged, seemed happier than the silver medalists.

Furthermore, people who watched interviews with many of these same athletes rated the silver medalists more negatively focused on finishing second rather than first. They rated the bronze medalist as more positively focused finishing third rather than fourth. For these athletes (bronze medalists), feelings of satisfaction were based more on their thoughts of what might have been than on the reality of what was.

When Describing Your Friends and Foes

Describing friends and foes is always an easy task. We intend to produce favorable impression about our friends. Similarly, we try to generate unfavorable impression about foes. The task is more challenging when our targets are our best friends or worst enemies.

Generally, people use adjectives and descriptors to create favourable or unfavorable impression of others. But the basic dilemma involves the number and intensity of descriptors. Some people are led to behave that the number matters. Greater is the number of descriptors (adjectives), deeper is the impact. While describing their best chosen friends, they present an elaborate list of adjectives. They may use adjectives such as honest, hardworking, sincere, punctual, reticent, and so on. Similarly, they use a long list of adjectives to describe their foes. They may say that their foes are lazy, insincere, cheat, dishonest, and so on. Briefly they are guided by a principle technically known as *summation model*.

Contrary to this belief, research has shown that the real functional principle is the *average model*. When we describe persons, listeners and readers seem to use a mental algebra. The listeners and readers sum up the intensity of positive (or negative) feeling tone of all adjectives and divide the sum by the number of adjectives.

For the sake of illustration, a case can be cited. Suppose Person 1 intends to generate a very favourable impression about his/her friend. Let us say Person 1 uses five adjectives such as punctual, meticulous, clean, competitive and sympathetic while describing his/her friend (individual X). Assuming that there adjectives carry 4, 3, 2, 3, and 4 units of favourable impression, the intended positive impression happens to the 16 units of positive impression (presuming that the units vary from 1 to 7). On the contrary, Person 2 intends similar effect but uses only two adjectives: honest and sincere (for individual X). Presuming that the descriptor honest and sincere carry 7 and 5 units of positive impression, its sum would be 12 units. Accordingly, a more positive impression would be formed about X, if summation model works. But a more positive impression would be formed about Y if average model works since $\frac{7+5}{2}$ is greater that $\frac{4+3+2+3+4}{5}$. Experience and research indicates that average model is functional.

What is the most important tip for you? If you really want to generate very positive impression about your friend, use strong adjectives but a small number of adjectives. Similarly, while putting your foe in an unfavourable position, use a small number of strong negative adjectives. You can beat your competitor if you follow this simple rule of mental algebra.

Planning Fallacy

Time budgeting is an essential part of our planned activities. Goals may be small or large. But people in modern times do a lot of planning to achieve the goal. While planning, they not only chalk out the work methods, they also stipulate limited time to reach the target. An interesting observation in this context involves the tendency to underestimate the amount of time needed for the work.

A work may require fifteen days, but people presume that they would be able to complete within ten days. An assignment may require four/five months, but they hope to complete within a couple of months. This human weakness, known as *planning fallacy,* characterizes all categories of people.

Why does this happen? There are two possible explanations. First, it is observed that people are motivated to complete. This motivation to complete makes them optimistic, sometimes over-optimistic. Because of over-optimism, they view their capacity in unrealistic terms and estimate a shorter time duration.

Second, people's attention is more focused on future than on past, while estimating the required time, people need to be realistic. They need to consider and evaluate their past performance. What are the different kinds of work they have undertaken in the past? What are the specific types of work where they have managed to complete? What are the particular areas where they have failed miserably in keeping to the time? Work and time analysis would be very helpful in making decision about the upcoming tasks.

Unfortunately, people do not make such analysis of their past success and failure. Consequently, they are likely to make mistakes in estimating work-time.

In order to avoid planning fallacy, self-evaluation is essential. When a person openly examines his/her past performance, he/she becomes realistic and makes accurate estimation of the required time.

On Loneliness

How many people are tormented by loneliness? It is very difficult to have a precise answer to this question. Many people assume that the loneliest age group is the elderly. However, others believe that adolescents are more lonely than the elderly. The difficulty of giving precise estimate arises from the fact that the nature of loneliness is complex.

Loneliness occurs when a person has fewer interpersonal relationships than desired or when these interpersonal relationships are not as rewarding as desired. Of course people vary in their needs for social interactions. If individuals are not distressed by the quality and quantity of their social and emotional ties, they do not feel lonely.

There are several ways to think about loneliness. *Emotional loneliness* springs from an absence of an intimate attachment figure. A child may feel lonely because of the separation from mother. A person may experience emotional loneliness owing to the loss of spouse. *Social isolation* stems from the lack of friendship networks. Persons moving into a new city initially experience social loneliness, although emotional loneliness does not result. Similarly, with loss of a spouse, a person experiences emotional loneliness, even if social isolation has not occurred.

Emotional loneliness is basically tied to the absence of an intimate partner. Social loneliness results from many sources, depending on age. In college students, it is the *quantity* of friendship contacts. In the older group, it is the *quality* of contacts. It is also important to recognize that social support can't compensate for emotional loneliness. This is not to say that social support is unimportant. But it is important to recognize that different types of loneliness require different patterns of coping.

Another way to look at loneliness is in terms of its duration. *Transient loneliness* involves brief and sporadic feelings of loneliness. *Transitional loneliness* occurs when people who have had satisfying social relationships in the past become lonely because of a specific disruption of their social network (death of a loved one or moving to a now city). *Chronic loneliness* is a condition that adversely affects people over a period of years.

It is not difficult to identify roots of loneliness. A key problem seems to be early negative social behaviour that leads to rejection by friends and teachers. Children who are aggressive or withdrawn are likely to suffer peer rejection. Some children develop social behaviour (aggression, aloofness, competitiveness) that lead to rejection by adults and peers. A vicious cycle gets set up on which a child's inappropriate behaviour prompts rejection by others, which in turn triggers negative expectation about social interaction in the child, along with more negative behaviour and so on. To help break this self-defeating cycle, it is crucial to help children learn appropriate social skills early in life.

Without intervention, insecurely attached children can grow into insecurely attached adults. Insecure attachment is correlated with loneliness in adults. Stated differently, people who are anxious and who do not love others experience high levels of loneliness. People who avoid others are likely to experience moderate levels of loneliness. People showing secure attachment (loving others) are likely to experience the least of loneliness.

Social commentators and psychologists are concerned about recent trends that seems to be undermining social connections in our contemporary life. Working mothers and fathers may be so pressed for time that they have little time to cultivate intimate relationships. Because of busy schedules, face-to-face interaction at home are reduced as family members eat in front of the TV. People watch the television so much that meaningful family conversation is reduced. While technology makes life easier in some respects and does provide opportunity for meaningful relationships, it has its down sides. These trends are to be seriously considered in the context of combating loneliness.

Conquering Loneliness

For people who are chronically lonely, painful feelings are a fact of life. Three factors that figure in chronic loneliness are shyness, poor social skill, and a self-defeating explanatory style. Of course, the link between these factors and loneliness could go either way. Feeling lonely might cause one to experience shyness, but feeling shyness can also lead to loneliness.

Shyness is commonly associated with loneliness. Shyness refers to discomfort, inhibition, and excessive caution in interpersonal relations. Shy people are timid about expressing themselves. They are overly self-conscious about how other are reacting to them. They embarrass easily. They also experience physiological symptoms of their anxiety, such as a racing pulse, blushing or an upset stomach.

Studies have found that lonely people evaluate others negatively, although this is not always the case. People experiencing chronic loneliness typically have casual acquaintances rather than close friends. They spend much of their time in solitary activities such as listening to music or reading.

Often these individuals are adults who were unable

to break out of self-defeating pattern of social behaviour developed early in life. Lonely people show lower responsiveness to their conversational partner and are self-focused. Similarly, they are inhibited and unassertive. They speak less than non-lonely people. They seem to disclose less about themselves than those who are not lonely.

It is easy to see how repeated rejections can foster negative expectation about social interaction. Thus, lonely people are prone to irrational thinking about their social skills. Unfortunately, once people develop these negative ideas, they often behave in ways to confirm their expectation. This sets up a vicious cycle of behaviour.

Psychologists have pointed out that lonely people engage in *negative self-talk* that prevents them from pursuing intimacy in an active and positive manner. Some clusters of ideas underlying these faulty explanatory styles can be identified. The faulty tendency is to attribute loneliness to *stable causes* (the causes that seem to be permanent). Similarly, the faulty tendency is to attribute loneliness to *internal causes* (causes that are associated with the person, not with the environment). This constitutes a self-defeating attributional (explanatory) style. In other words, lonely people tell themselves that they are lonely because they are basically unlovable individuals. Not only is this a devastating belief, it is also self-defeating because it offers no way to change the situation.

The personal consequences associated with chronic loneliness can be painful and sometimes over whelming: low self-esteem, hostility, depression, alcoholism, psychosomatic illness, and possibly, suicide. Although there are no simple solutions to loneliness, there are some effective ones.

One option is to use Internet to overcome loneliness, although this approach can be a two-edged sword. The positive side, the Internet is an obvious boon to busy people. Moreover, shy people can interact without anxiety associated with face-to-face conversation. But if lonely people spend a lot of time online, this may drastically cut down the amount of face-face-face communication. Hence, a balance is to be maintained in this context.

A second suggestion is to avoid the temptation to withdraw from social situations. When lonely, must people prefer to listen music or to read books. It used occasionally, reading and listening to music can be constructive ways of dealing with loneliness. However, as long-term strategies, they do not help lonely people to acquire "real world friends". So a balance has to the maintained.

A third strategy is to break out of the habit of self-defeating explanatory style. It is improper to use stable (causes that last for ever) and internal (causes that are associated with the person) factors as causes of loneliness. People have to develop the habit of explaining loneliness in terms of unstable (temporary) factors and external (environmental) factors. For example, a person may say to himself/herself that he/she is experiencing lonely primarily because he/she has come to a new city and his/her loneliness would soon pass off. The tendency to explain loneliness in terms of external (environmental/situational) and temporary factors would be helpful to combat loneliness.

Finally, to thwart loneliness development of social skills is very crucial. There is a number of skills designated as interpersonal skills. The ability to decode nonverbal causes in others, conversational skills, skills to disclose oneself and assertive communication skills are example of such interpersonal skills. It is suggested that these skills be learned ad maintained for effectively dealing with loneliness.

Cluster of cognitions typical of lonely people

Clusters	Cognitions	Behaviours
A	1. I'm undesirable. 2. I'm dull and boring.	Avoidance of friendship
B	1. I can't communicate with other people. 2. My thoughts and feelings are bottled up inside.	Low self-disclosure
C	1. I'm not a good lover in bed. 2. I can't relax, be spontaneous, and enjoy sex.	Avoidance of sexual relationships
D	1. I can't seem to get what I want from this relationship. 2. I can't say how I feel, or he/she might leave me.	Lack of relationships
E	1. I won't risk being hurt again. 2. I'd screw up any relationship.	Avoidance of potentially intimate relationships.
F	1. don't know how to act in this situation. 2. I'll make a fool of myself	Avoidance of other people

The Benefits of Togetherness

No man is an island. We live in a society and social connections provide the grease to the wheels of our lives. However, some people become lonely for one reason or the other. The hazards are expressed both in physiological terms (high blood pressure, loss of sleep, etc) and psychological forms (depression, anxiety).

There are many studies to document the health hazards of loneliness. Spiegel (1998), a Stanford University Professor, arranged support groups for women with advanced breast cancer. Regular group meetings and contacts were arranged. The meetings provided a forum through which they could talk about their problems and release their emotion. It was expected that the women would be relieved of their stress. The expectation was confirmed. But there was something else that was not initially expected. The women lived, 18 months more than women who did not have such support groups. Spiegel (1998) concluded: "The added survived time was longer than any medication or any medical treatment could be expected to provide for women with breast cancer so far advanced".

In another survey in California of the USA, data were obtained from 7000 residents. It was shown that those who lived alone died two to three times greater than those with much social contact. Similarly, another study based on data obtained from people visiting doctors indicate the benefits of togetherness. It is found that people with friends are two to three times less likely to die within nine to twelve years than those who do not have friends.

Research findings do suggest that married people are more likely than those who are unmarried to survive cancer for five years. Similarly, people who have a heart attack are less likely to have a second one if they live with someone than if they live alone. Amongst students buried in school work, and among the spouses of cancer patients more social support is associated with a stronger immune response. Based on multiple studies, some researchers have concluded that in times of stress, having social support lowers blood pressure, lessons stress hormones, and strengthens immune response.

The advantage of social contact is not restricted to humans. Pets provide company and this may play a useful role in dealing with loneliness. In a study, over a thousand individuals sixty-five years of age or older were asked whether they owned a pet. The number of negative events experienced in the previous six months were also assessed. Participants then reported every two months for a year on how many times they have contacted a physician. Among people with many negative life events, those with pet dogs has lower contacts with physicians.

A basic element in togetherness involves emotional release. With friends around, a person may cry, laugh, show and do a lot of things. It provides an effective out-let for pent-up emotion.

Although value of social support is widely accepted, there is no consensus with respect to the measurement of togetherness. In a large number of studies, social support is defined by the *number of social contact* a person has. This measure is predictive, but a simple social contact model has some limitations. One is that it glosses over the fact that people who are stuck in bad social relationships are more distressed, not less. Even good social relationship can heighten stress–particularly in women, who tend to do more of the "caring". An excessive attention to either one's own well-being or that of others increases health risks for men and women alike. A more balanced perspective is healthier. Second, having too many contacts may reduce the level of support.

A second model emphasizes, the quality of social support rather than quantity. The *intimacy model* predicts than the key is to have a close relation with a significant other. A third approach defines social support in terms of its *preferred availability*. The availability element offers a strong belief system to the individual that friends are available as and when necessary.

Despite the variation in the definition of social support, the benefits of togetherness is well-documented. It is further asserted that the spiral of togetherness is a basic strength in Indian society. Many experts have suggested the idea of constructing the orphanages and old age homes in close physical proximity. In Maharashtra, this plan has taken concrete shapes. This is a unique way of uniting two lonely groups (the very young and the very old) to reestablish the linkage and reinforce togetherness.

Bury Your Worries

The killers of yester years are no longer the killers of human beings in modern times. The epidemics and infections diseases that threatened human life in the past have receded to the periphery. The modern villains that have appeared on the center stage are problems of relationship. Furthermore, problems of relationship spread virus of worries. Worries surely and slowly destroy human happiness.

However, a small and occasional worry does not cause catastrophic loss. It is the intensity and chronicity of worry which cause substantial damage.

People need to know the dynamics of human response. Why do some people worry a lot for considerable amount of time while others manage to limit its spread. It has been clearly shown that the genesis of worry is the faulty thought pattern.

There are *three* distinct ways in which thought patterns may go astray. First, there may be *magnification*. The worrying person magnifies an event, especially bad (negative) event to an exaggerated proportion. Suppose a person arranges a party and it fails. This may be a very small event in comparison to the total life scheme of a person.

Yet, the person analyzes the error beyond proportion. Why was it failure? The person considers all farfetched causes. May be he/she did not invite guests properly. May be that he/she does not possess minimum skills to arrange a party. Further, the person may think that some people have plotted to spoil the party. On the basis of this event of failure, the person draws conclusion regarding his abilities, skills, personality and what not.

The tendency to magnify the negative event brings problem. Too much analysis brings paralysis. The person blames himself/herself. A sense of guilt cripples the person.

Second, *minimization* is another faulty pattern that damages the mental health. While trivial things are magnified, important things are slighted. The person undertakes an assignment that demands care and caution. Yet, the person does not attach priority to it and becomes neglectful. The minimization of its importance leads to failure (or sloppy performance). Consequently the person becomes victim of harsh criticism and insults are hurled at him/her. This results in subsequent worries for which there is no repair.

Third, the tendency for drawing *arbitrary inference* is a faulty thinking style. In a gathering, people may laugh and dance in the process of merry-making. But a worry-prone person may feel that others are taunting him or her. Because of the tendency of arbitrary inference, the person does not see "the connection where it exists. But the person "invents" a connection where there is none. Such habits make the person unnecessarily depressive.

Thus, negative moods are the product of negative and faulty thoughts. Individual wishing to bury their worries have to develop the habit of giving up their negative and defective thinking styles. They have to combat worries by joining three sides of a healthy triangle.

1. Draw the first line by avoiding unnecessary magnification of small event.
2. Draw the second line by avoiding minimization (avoid trivializing) of significant events.
3. Draw the haze line try making right connection between behavioural causes and outcomes. Do not draw arbitrary inference.

Avoid magnification of small events

Avoid minimization of big events

Avoid arbitrary inference

Avoid Faulty Explanatory Styles

Accidents do happen even in well-regulated lives. Yet, they do not produce similar consequences in lives of different persons. For some persons, it leads to disastrous outcomes, whereas it has negligible negative effective for others. A few others may also derive some benefits out of these negative (bad) events. It has been shown that the main mediating mechanism that brings a difference is the explanatory styles an individual adopts.

When people face bad events, they generally ask *three* fundamental questions to themselves. People differ with respect to the kind of answers they present for themselves. These explanations shape their basic adaptation.

First, people encountering bad events ask the question: *Who is responsible for the event?* Some people feel that they themselves are responsible for the bad event and for their failure to escape the accident. If they blame themselves fully, depression is the likely outcome. They feel a loss of self-confidence. They consider that they are inept. On the contrary, other people may think that external circumstances and other people are responsible for the event. In this case, guilt and self-blame is avoided. Suppose a person arranges a party and people do not turn up. In this context, they may consider the possibility that people's absence is due to bad weather. On the other hand, people considering the possibility that they are not competent to arrange party feel very depressed. Thus, the intensity of depression is directly proportional to self-blame.

Second, people ask another question: *How long would the event continue?* At one extreme, people may consider bad (negative) events permanent. At the other extreme, people may regard bad events as temporary happening. Of course there are people occupying intermediate positions. It is observed that people explaining bad events in permanent terms experience chronic depression, whereas people considering bad events very fragile experience depression very briefly. In other words, it is advisable to view bad events as temporary phenomena. People may say to themselves: The clouds would soon pass and we would have bright sun shine.

Individuals also ask a third fundamental question to themselves. *How global is the effect of bad event?* Suppose a person meets an accident and loses a hand. In this situation, the person may feel that his/her life has been doomed. The total life is damaged. Thus the explanatory style is global. On the contrary, another person in the same situation may think that he/she has lost a hand but other organs are alright. It is possible to do many things with the use of other limbs. It can be observed that global explanation makes depression very pervasive. The person spills over his/her depression to other areas of life. On the contrary, the person who uses specific explanation limits his/her depression to a single area.

In sum, the explanatory styles using self-blame, stability and globality heighten depression. On the contrary, the explanations using external causal explanation, unstable time explanation and specific attribution reduce depression greatly.

It is also important to suggest that people need to use the reverse mode while explaining good events. If they use internal explanation, they think of their roles in positive events. This brings happiness. Similarly they need to stretch the cause of good events over time. In addition, their tendency to spill over the good outcome to other areas of life would bring positive effects. For happiness, people need to use internal, permanent and global factors for explaining good events.

5. You give an important talk in front of a group and the audience reacts negatively.	7 6 5 4 3 2 1	1 2 3 4 5 6 7	1 2 3 4 5 6 7
6. You do a project which is highly praised.	7 6 5 4 3 2 1	1 2 3 4 5 6 7	1 2 3 4 5 6 7
7. You meet a friend who acts hostilely towards you.	7 6 5 4 3 2 1	1 2 3 4 5 6 7	1 2 3 4 5 6 7
8. You don't get all the work done that others expect of you.	7 6 5 4 3 2 1	1 2 3 4 5 6 7	1 2 3 4 5 6 7
9. Your spouse has been treating you more lovingly.	7 6 5 4 3 2 1	1 2 3 4 5 6 7	1 2 3 4 5 6 7
10. You apply for a position that you want badly and you get it.	7 6 5 4 3 2 1	1 2 3 4 5 6 7	1 2 3 4 5 6 7
11. Go out on holidays and it goes badly.	7 6 5 4 3 2 1	1 2 3 4 5 6 7	1 2 3 4 5 6 7
12. You get a promotion.	7 6 5 4 3 2 1	1 2 3 4 5 6 7	1 2 3 4 5 6 7

Scoring : Note that item numbers 1,3,6,9,10 & 12 represent positive events; other items denote negative events. Sum your ratings across items number 1,3,6,9, & 10, 12 per question. Then sum them across all threee questions. Lower the sum the better. Similarity sum your ratings across item no 2,4,5,7,8 and 11. Higher the score the better.

13. Interpretation

Scores	For Negative Events	For Positive Events
Below 36	Low helplessness(Competence)	Very low wellness
37-72	Moderate helplessness	Moderate wellness
73-108	High helplessness	High wellness
Above 108	Very high helplessness	Very high wellness

Perceiving Control: An Essential Stop Towards Successful Ageing

The process of ageing, though inevitable, does not pose a threat to all individuals. Of course, many people become quite anxiety-ridden and scared at the thought of approaching old age. A few others get prepared to encounter its challenge. Still a few others feel confident to cope with it.

It has been shown that an important mind set that helps in this context is the perception of control. It is true that a part of the old age problems stems from the physical decay the person experiences. The decline in the capacity to see and hear, for example, brings a considerable amount of unhappiness. The aged person feels handicapped in these areas of sensory capabilities. But other part of the problem springs from the perception that the individuals are losing control over their immediate environment. No body consult them about important decisions adopted in the family. They are not asked about the kind of food they would like to have. They are not asked about specific visitors to be invited for a family ceremony. No body seeks their opinion about the piece of land to be purchased for the family.

Consequently, they experience a sense of uncontrollability in their immediate environment.

A beautiful study illustrated this point. A researcher with a group of volunteers went to two hospitals where elderly persons are taken care of. In the first hospital, he gave out an information that a group of volunteers (high school students) would come to the hospital and render service to them. They would clean the hospital surroundings, change the bed, take them to toilets and would assist them in various forms. They would be available seven hours a week. Then the researcher gave a day-wise schedule (For example, 2 p.m. to 3 p.m. on Monday, 10 a.m. to 11 a.m. on Tuesday, so on) for each week. The researcher told also similar things with one major change in the second hospital. He handed over the phone number of the leader of the volunteer group and asked patients to indicate their needs to the hospital authorities with a request to inform the leader telephonically. It was of course indicated that the volunteer service would be restricted to seven hours a week. This programme continued for several months in both the hospitals.

It is easy to surmise that the arrangements were almost same in both hospitals except one major aspect. In the first hospitals, the elderly patients had *no control* over the time of service availability. The volunteers used to come and go at their appointed hours. In contrast, patients in the second hospital could control timings depending on their needs. They could ask for service when needed. The researcher evaluated the consequences. He arranged to measure the improvement both on physiological and psychological induces. Physiological indices included the gain or loss of weight, blood pleasure, amount of sleep, regularity of bowl movement and other indicators. With respect to psychological indices of mental health, they were asked to indicate the extent of their worry, happiness, zest for living and similar mental states. As I predicted, individuals in second hospital showed greater degree of health as measured by both physiological and psychological indicators. The study documented the positive effects of perceiving control in the environment.

In order to study the impact of enhanced control, another researcher attempted an intervention. In a geriatric hospital, he arranged a programme. The elderly patients who were not too weak were trained to plant the trees in the hospital garden. They regularly watered the plants for a number of months. Their attention was also drawn to the positive changes taking place in the garden. It was indicated to them that the growth, the leafing and the flowering were die to *their efforts*. The knowledge of results of their action was clearly communicated to them. Compared to the changes taking place in a similar hospital without such arrangement, the elderly persons indicated significant improvement in their physical and mental health.

Thus, a clear-cut suggestion is imparted with respect to planned intervention. It is posited that our planned activities to enhance the perception of control of elderly persons would be very helpful in promoting their health.

Roots of Achievement Orientation

The progress and prosperity of a nation depends on the efforts of achievement oriented individuals. Starting from the cotton factory to computer industry, the success story of an organization is incomplete without mention of achievement description of a single or a few individuals. The fundamental question concerns: where does achievement striving come from? Research suggests that early childhood socialization is a key factor although life experiences do contribute to its growth.

Quite sometime ago, a researcher got interested in finding out the genesis of achievement orientation. She observed a large number of children and split them into two categories (high-achieving and low-achieving) on the basis of their behaviour. She then met the mothers of these two categories of children and asked a number of simple questions. The questions included the following?

- At what age you would allow your child to cross the road independently?
- At what age would you allow your child to play with scissors?
- At what age would you allow your child to go to the school independently?

- At what age would you allow your child to play with match sticks?

There were other questions of similar nature. For every question, mothers of high achieving children indicated a lower age level compared with the report of mothers of low-achieving children. It clearly posits that mothers of achieving children offer a greater degree of *independence training* than do mothers of low-achieving children. In contrast, mothers of low achieving children are more protective than mothers of high achieving children.

Apart from independence training offered to children, another element was also observed. It was shown that mothers of achieving children express their *warmth in an explicit manner.* Whenever such children report their achievements to their parents, the parents embrace the child or show some form of positive physical gesture. Children's achievement gets accepted in the form of a physical demonstration. It is not enough that parents feel happy and implicitly thank. The physical expression of parental warmth, especially the mother's warmth, is a necessary stimulus for future growth of achievement orientation.

Finally, parents can do a lot by setting examples of high standard of performance. Both the parents or one of the parents may be role model for the child. The child may get an opportunity to witness excellent standards of performance try observing his or parents Alternately the child may be exposed to stories containing heroic deeps of other persons. It is told that Shivaji's mother used to tell stories of heroic achievements borrowed from the great epics. Similarly, it has been documented that the mother of Rishi Modi, the former General Managers of Tata Group of Industries, used to tell him stories of great achievements.

Thus, the early socialization process plays a very significant role. The independence training, physical expression of parental warmth, and exposure to standards of excellence provide the building blocks on which the edifice of achievement is constructed subsequently.

The Urge to Achieve

The striving to seek, to find and to achieve is a special type of human ability. The appropriate form of socialization during early child-hood period contributes to its germination. Subsequently a stimulating and competitive atmosphere fosters it. The resulting achievement motivation not only brings fruits of individual growth and prosperity; it also leads to collective efficacy.

Although it is not difficult to identify achievement-oriented individuals in our vicinity, it is useful to delineate their characteristics. The recognition of these characteristics helps us to promote and provide support system in our environment.

First, persons high on achievement strivings *take moderate levels of risk*. Unlike conservatives, they do not avoid risks: they are also not like gamblers going for a very high levels of risk. It can be easily demonstrated in the form of a ring-tossing game. For instance, a ball can be placed on the top of a table and individuals could be asked to toss a ring that would encircle the ball. Individuals could be further allowed to choose their own distances from the table. If closely observed, it may be seen that a few individuals would take a conservative stand. They would stand very close to the table so that they are successful almost all the time. Similarly, a number of persons may stand at a farther place resulting in a rare success. Their gambler-like attempt may bring only 5 to 10% of success.

Some of the individuals would choose distances where probability of success ranges from 40% to 60%. This moderate level of risk characterizes achievement-oriented individuals. They prefer to take risk, yet they avoid an extreme levels of risk. The task which is challenging keeps them involved.

Second, achievement oriented individuals display persistence. They do not easily give up. In other words, an encounter with obstacles intensify their efforts. It is interesting to observe that frustration, especially mild frustration, has two different types of effects. Some people, while faced with frustration, give up and become depressed. But some other people become more serious and intensify their efforts. They become more determined. Achievement-oriented individuals follow the latter course. They demonstrate long-term persistence.

Third, achievement-oriented individuals seek immediate and performance-related feedback. Suppose someone is a teacher. If such a teacher is achievement-oriented, he or she would expect feedback from the target persons (students). It would not make him or her very happy if described as a very good person or an excellent individual. The achievement-oriented teacher would seek performance-related feedback. The person would like to know the areas (such as content coverage, organization, relevance and originality) where he/she is going strong. Similarly, he/she would like to know the domains of his/her weakness. Furthermore, the person would seek these domain-specific feedback (knowledge of results) to modify the performance.

Finally, it has been observed that achievement-oriented persons express their happiness at the time of accomplishment. They are not indifferent to moments of success. They express positive affects in an explicit manner. There may be individual variation in the extent of expressing joy. But physical gestures and positive affects are explicitly shown.

Developing an Assertive Communication Style

Many people have a hard time being assertive. However, this problem is more common among females because they are socialized to be more submissive than males. Women are expected to be "nice" and "soft spoken". Consequently, assertiveness training is especially popular among women. Men too, find assertiveness raining helpful, because some men have been socialized to be passive and others want to learn to be less aggressive and more assertive.

Assertiveness involves acting in your own best interest by expressing your thoughts and feelings directly and honestly. Essentially, assertiveness involves standing up for your own rights when someone else is about to infringe on them.

The nature of assertive communication is best understood by contrasting it with other types of communication. *Submissive communication* involves consistently giving in to others on points of possible contention. Submissive people let others take advantage of them. Typically, their biggest problem is that they cannot say no to unreasonable request. A common example is the person who cannot ask his or her roommate to tone down the noisy sound of the television.

Although roots of excessive submissiveness have not been investigated fully, they appear to lie in excessive concern for gaining social approval of others. However, the feeling of pushed aside lead to withdrawing, sulking and crying.

At the other end of the spectrum, *aggressive communication* involves saying and getting what you want, but at the expense of others feeling and rights. With assertive behaviour, you strive to respect others rights and defend your own. Assertive communication appears to be more adaptive than either submissive communication or aggressive communication. Submissive communication leads to poor self-worth, self-denial and strained interpersonal relationship. Aggressive communication leads to guilt and disharmony. In contrast, assertive communication fosters high self-esteem, satisfactory interpersonal relationship and effective conflict management.

In order to develop assertive communication style, it is helpful to follow a sequence of activities as a form of training.

1. **Understand assertive communication style.** To produce assertive behaviour, you need to understand what it looks and sounds like. One way to accomplish this is to imagine situations calling for assertiveness and compare hypothetical submissive, assertive and aggressive responses.

2. **Monitor your assertive communication.** Most people's communication varies from one situation to situation. They are assertive in some situations, while they are submissive in other situations. You can observe

the conditions (factors, persons, and so on) that make you less empowered. Once you monitor, you would be able to combat submissiveness.

3. **Observe a model's assertive communication.** Try to spot and identify a role mode in the context of assertive communication. When you are successful in identifying a model, you can observe very closely. You can notice his or her style of self-presentation, conservational style and expression modality. You may find out the ways in which the model dissents. The model would be a source of information as well as a source of inspiration. If a model is not available, another option is to see through self-improvement books.

4. **Practice assertive communication.** The key to achieving assertive communication is to practice and work toward gradual improvement. Your practice can take several forms. In covert rehearsal you can imagine a situation requiring assertive communication and frame dialogues. In real-life role playing, you can ask your friend or trainer to play the role of an antagonist. Some experts suggest the idea of *shaping*. You count the number of assertive communication you have produced today Plan to increase the number tomorrow. A systematic and conscious effort to increase the frequency of assertive communication would be helpful.

5. **Adopt an assertive attitude.** Most of the assertiveness training programme are tailored for specific situations. However, real life situations rarely match the hypothetical situations used in training programme. Hence, it is suggested that people need to develop an overall life style attitude to deal with. A change in attitude is probably crucial to achieving flexible assertive behaviour.

Are you unduly submissive?
Answer these questions: 'yes' or 'no'.
1. When someone ask you for a unreasonable favour, do you have difficulty saying no?
2. Do you feel timid about returning flawed merchandises?
3. Do you have hard time requesting even small favours from others?
4. When a group is hotly debating an issue, are you shy about speaking up?
5. When a sales person pressures you to buy something you don't want, is it hand for you to resist?

If you answer 'yes' to several of these questions you have unduly submissive. Take steps to develop assertive communication.

Power of Persuasion

No leader can succeed without matching the art of persuasion. But there is also science in that skill. There are *six* basic rules of winning friends and influencing people.

Rule of linking. People like those who like them. The important thing is to establish the bond early because it creates good will and trustworthiness in every subsequent encounter. Accordingly, you have to discover at least one common area of enjoyment. Once you discover it, you ca extend your love, affection, praise, and support. The attachment bond would strengthen the potency of your persuasive message on subsequent occasions.

Along with cultivating a fruitful relationship you can also praise to repair one that has been damaged in the past. It is quite possible that you do not like all aspects of a person. Yet, try hard to find something you could admire. Your admiration in his absence may also reach him or her through another person. You may find later that your enemy of yesterday is ready to comply with your request today.

Rule of reciprocity. Praise is likely to have a softening effect on humans. The human tendency is to treat people the way they treat him or her. If you have ever caught yourself smiling at a colleague just because he or she smiled first, you know how this principle works.

Charity rely on reciprocity. A charity organization using only a well-crafted fund-raising letter generated a very respectable 18% response to its appeal. But the organization started enclosing a small gift in the envelope; the response rate nearly doubled to 35%.

What works in that letter works in other forms too. Our greeting cards, birth-day wishes, social visits, congratulatory messages and other forms of well-wish establish a bond of reciprocity. Although gift-giving is one of the cruder applications of rule of reciprocity, people can use more sophisticated forms. These include a sense of trust a spirit of cooperation, a pleasant conversation and expression of gratitude.

Rule of social models. It is shown that people follow the lead of similar ones. People rely heavily on the people around them for cues on how to think, feel and act. Suppose a group of volunteers are collecting donations door-to-door for some charity purpose. If they display a list of neighbourhood residents who have already donated to the cause, it is very likely that the donor list would get longer.

To the people being solicited, the friends' and neighbours' names on the list are a form of social evidence about how they should respond. But the evidence would not be compelling if the names are those of random strangers. The persuasion becomes effective when the list includes the names of friends.

Rule of consistency. By and large, people tend to be consistent. Most people, once they take a stand or go on record in favour of a position, prefer to stick to it. Hence it is useful to make people's commitments active, public and voluntary. In a study, people were asked to give consent to using their names on a handout advocating safe driving in the locality. Many people gave their consent. Later they were requested to place a sign board appealing safe driving in front of their house. It was shown that compared with first time request, second time request to those who agreed to use their names on the handout produced higher incidence of compliance. Many of those who expressed commitments earlier to small request (use of name on handout) also expressed commitment to bigger request (placing the signboard in front of their houses).

Accordingly, it is advised that people need to be persuaded to make their compliance statements in the public.

Rule of authority. People defer to experts. In many walks of life, people are easily persuaded by experts. We change our health habits if advised by a doctor. A mathematics student uses a particular math formula if suggested by his or her professor. Considering the limit on time, people feel like following the advice of authority.

A basic implication of this principle suggests that it would no be wise to assume people know our expertise. Although it may not be ethical to boast about our credential, it is pragmatic to indicate our credibility prior to our persuasion message. This is why we have the convention of introducing a guest in a congregation before he or she makes presentation. The information relating to his or credential makes it easy to have persuasive impact.

Rule of scarcity. People want more of what they can have less of. It is a common experience that items and opportunity seem to be more valuable as they became less available. Accordingly, agents can harness the scarcity principle with the expressed emphasis on limited-item, limited-supply, and one-of-a-kind offer. For instance, the information that a special clinic has been set up after a long span of years and it would remain operative only for a limited period would draw a large number of target population.

While applying rules of persuasion, two important considerations are to be noted. First, the agent of change may find it useful to apply more than one rule. In other words, a combination of rules is likely to be very effective. Second, the techniques of persuasion must be used within the bounds of ethics. The personal value system of the individual as well as the professional ethics of a group provide normative boundaries within which rules of persuasion are used.

Rational Intelligence is not Enough

Success and intelligence have become synonymous in our common parlance. When students are successful in class-room situations, we call them intelligent. When employees in organizes outperform, we designate them intelligent. Similarly, intelligence is attributed to one's accomplishment when he or she registers success in his/her personal life. The word "intelligence" and its operational expression "intelligence quotient" (IQ) is offered as an all pervasive explanatory concept for life time achievement.

Prior to delineating the significance of IQ, it is useful to indicate the backdrop against which rational intelligence (IQ) was popularized. Long time ago teachers in schools of Paris faced a problem. They found that all categories of students in the class were not in a position to derive benefit from class-room instruction. They thought of a plan. In their view, it was necessary to classify students into specific categories of laggards, averages and achieving students. If they could be classified, it would be easy on the part of teachers to tailor instructions in accordance with students' receptivity.

Psychologists came to their rescue. Psychologists

first made an elaborate observation of skills a child shows at different age levels in a particular society (say French society). Accordingly, they prepared a list of skills one-year children show, two-year children show, and so on. On this basis, they prepared test materials for different age groups. This was indeed a clever trick. If a five-year old child could perform all the tests meant for a five-year old, he or she would be considered 'average'. If a five-year old child shows skills on test materials meant for a six or seven-year-old child, he or she would be regarded superior. On the contrary, if a five-year old child completes only a test meant for four-year old child, he or she would be considered low average.

The whole exercise was expressed in the form of a simple formula.

$$\text{Intelligence Quotient, (IQ)} = \frac{\text{Mental Age}}{\text{Chronological Age}} \times 100$$

Obviously, an IQ score of 100 implies that a boy or girl is average in his/her intellectual ability. If a child with an IQ score of 100 has chronological age ten, the mental age would also be ten. If the chronological age is 23 the mental age is also 23, in case of average IQ score of 100. On the other hand, an IQ score of 140 is indicative of the fact that a child of ten-year-old is performing the skills of a fourteen-year old child. Similarity, an IQ score of 80 would mean that a ten-year-old child is performing the skill of eight-year-old child.

Although the measurement of IQ and its application in school, college and work place has immensely helped us to make very good prediction of people's success, there have been some interesting development in recent years.

The works of neuropsychologists have revealed an interesting aspect. It has shown that human brain may be one, but there is duality in functions. The left part of the brain-left hemisphere-deals with logical and language functions. The right half of the brain-right hemisphere-deals with pattern recognition and emotion. Another finding is more interesting.

When the evolution of the species was in progress and the species were on the stage of reptiles, some ring-like structure began to form. Since 'limbus' is the Greek word for ring, specialists called it *limbic system'*. The limbic system took care of emotional responses. In terms of evolution, emotion came first. Subsequently the cortex –the higher-brain representing thinking centers –came to being. Since smell was important from survival point of view, 'nose centre' appeared in the thinking-brain. *In short, the brain has clearly two distinct parts: the feeling brain and the thinking brain. Furthermore, feeling brain is older than the thinking brain.*

Recent evidence has clearly shown that human development is dependent both on the cognitive and emotional development. The development of rational intelligence leads to lopsided development. The total success depends on both IQ and EQ. Since EQ has not been looked after in the past, it is urgent and necessary to develop EQ.

Several components of EQ have been identified. Our efforts need to be directed towards developing these components.

- **Self awareness**: Awareness of one's one strength and limitation
- **Social skills**: Interpersonal sensitivity including empathy

- **Self-control**: Control of one's emotion especially negative emotion such an anger and aggressiveness; Tolerance
- **Self-motivation**: High level of persistence
- **Positive mood**: Optimism and happiness.

Who is a Creative Individual?

Creative individuals and creative products are genuine treasures in this world. Although creative products in the domains of art, literature, science and technology receive public attention following widespread acceptance of the achievement, creative persons often encounter struggle and suffering. It is essential that creative children and adults are identified so that these budding achievers are encouraged during formative periods of their lives.

The proper identification of creative potential requires objective indicators. Fortunately, psychologists have identified *four* indicators of creative pursuits. It is relatively easy to offer illustration of these indicators in the context of children.

Suppose we ask a simple question; In how many ways can you use a piece of brick? It is a common experience to find that children would answer differently. Let us imagine the following response patterns of two different children.

Child-1	Child-2
1. To build a house	1. To build an office
2. To build a school	2. To use it as a paper weight
3. To build a store	3. To write something on the wall
4. To build a stable	4. To drive away a cat
5. To build a temple	5. To use it as a door-block

The analysis of the responses of these two children generates fascinating features. First, the *fluency* is an indicator of creativity. It refers to the amount of ideas generated per unit time. It is shown that both the children have presented five ideas. Each of these two children may be awarded a score of 5 for fluency.

The second indicator of creativity is the *flexibility*- the number of thought categories. Although both of the children have produced 5 ideas each, the ideas generated by the first child belong to the single category of building something. In contrast, the second child's ideas represent separate thought categories. Hence, Child-1 is supposed to obtain a score of 1 for flexibility whereas Child-2 is credited with a score of 5 for flexibility.

The notion of flexibility requires a bit elaboration. Infact this is a very important element of creative work, it art, literature or science. Flexibility reflects divergent thinking which is at the root of creative process. In *convergent thinking*, all thoughts are directed towards a single point. In contrast, thoughts are directed towards different points in divergent thinking. It is important to recognize that divergent thinking is the crux of creative process.

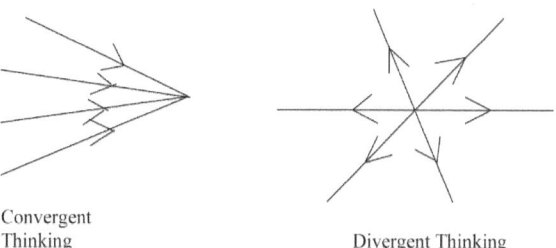

Convergent Thinking   Divergent Thinking

Third, creative children not only demonstrate flexible thought patterns, they are also capable of elaborating their thought contents. They form new associations and elaborate and expand on these ideas.

Finally, the fourth most important indicator of creativity happens to be *originality*-the uncommonness of response. Statistically speaking an uncommon response is one that has less probability of being evoked. Let us consider the above example. It is observed that the responses of Child-2 regarding the use of brick is very unusual. If the same question is asked to 100 children, a very few children would answer the way the child-2 has answered. Because of such low incidence of occurrence, it is considered original. The child is credited with high scores for originality.

However, only statistical unusualness would not define originality. A drunken person's delirium may be very unusual. Such person may utter obscene words that others would hesitate to speak. Such words would not be considered original, even it these are unusual. The *social utility* factor has to be taken into consideration. A mad man's delirium, though unusual, does not contribute to social well-being. Hence it does not justify for claim for being a creative product.

In sum, fluency, flexibility, elaboration, and originality constitute criteria of creativity. These are operational and measurable. The measurement of creativity in terms of fluency, flexibility and originality is manifest not only in the context of usual-unusual tests (e.g., asking children to indicate the ways in which a piece of brick, a piece of paper, a piece of chalk, etc can be used), but also by other tests. Needless to say, creativity score is the sum total of scores across fluency, flexibility and originality indicators. The higher is the score, more creative is the person.

Another interesting technique to measure creativity

Consequences Test Children, even adults, can be asked to provide brief description indicating possible consequences of some unusual events. Below are given some illustration questions.

What would happen, if_ _____
1. schools have wheels_____?
2. people do not have to eat_____?
3. we would understand the language of tigers___?
4. man could roar _____?
5. man could walk on water_____?

As with the Usual-Unusual Test (e.g., In how many ways, can you use a piece of brick?), it is possible to generate fluency, flexibility and originality score of an individual. Creativity score is the sum total of scores across these three indicators.

Are Intelligent Persons Creative?

A large number of people have confusion regarding the relationship between intelligence and creativity. Intelligence refers to adaptive skills. It is ability to cope with environmental demands and pressures. Creativity, on the contrary, is the ability to produce something beautiful. Although these two abilities are related, the extent of this correlation is much less than what is popularly believed.

A longtime ago, a British psychologist made a formidable attempt to examine the correlation (relationship) between the two. He made an approximate quantification of scientific achievements of the-then-living scientists. This was possible in form of measuring the impact of a scientific invention as well as by examining the extent of citation (how many other scientists quote or cite this particular scientist). Similarly, the psychologist also measured intelligence of these scientists.

With quantitative data generated for both intelligence and creativity, the psychologist computed a statistical index called correlation coefficient. It was shown that the mean correlation was .4. It implied that only 16% (square of .4) of the variation in creativity can be accounted for by intelligence. In other words, intelligence contributes to a smaller proportion of creative behaviour.

Why is it so? A common sense explanation can be offered. It is generally observed that may intelligent persons are highly critical. When they encounter new ideas, they "see" many weak points. Their over-critical attitude prevents them from working on the new idea and do something constructive. Creative people, on the contrary, seize upon a now idea despite some inherent weakness in it. As a result, their creative pursuit leads them to "new finds". This explains as to why there is only a weak relation between intelligence and creativity.

The observation carries hopes and optimism for creative persons. In order to be creative, you don't have to be highly intelligence. A moderate level of intelligence would be necessary but you can enter the kingdom of creativity without much brilliance.

Further to this discussion, another element deserves our attention. It is important to recognize that motivation also plays a crucial role. Creative thoughts in the form divergent ideas may come and go... But such creative efforts take a tangible reality only in association with intense motivation. What we term talent in our common parlance is a combination of *three* resources: Intellectual, creative, and motivation. This can be schematically represented. The representation clearly shows the overlap and relationship amongst these three resources.

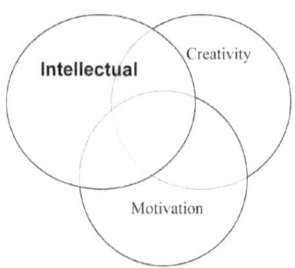

Becoming Creative

Becoming a creative person is aspiration of many people, but achievement of a few individuals. It has been discussed elsewhere that *divergent thinking* is the hall-mark of creative process. A creative person thinks in a flexible manner. One would be curious to know the techniques of developing divergent ways of thinking. In the formalized method of stimulating creativity, psychologists have made use of three major techniques. When we understand the basic principles underlying these three techniques, we can make use of them at an informal and individual level.

Brain Storming. In order to stimulate creativity and generate divergent solutions, the method of brain storming was popularized during war periods. The brain storming training sessions can be organized for children as well as for adults. The brain storming session consists of two stages: a green light stage and a red light stage.

During green light stage, the leader (or the coordinator) of the session presents the problem and seek solution alternatives. The essential feature of the green light stage involves an evaluation-free atmosphere. The leader assures the participating members that no criticism would be directed to any person. Participants may suggest very unusual and far-fetched solutions. The method is called brain storming, because there is free-wheeling of thoughts. People work under a criticism-free environment.

An illustration would bring further clarity to the concept. For example, the leader (coordinator) may ask children to suggest different ways of preparing a cup of tea. A particular child may respond to the problem in an unusual way. He/she may suggest that a pot would be placed on the ground and milk would be poured from the roof top. Although the solution sounds like the Birbal story, nobody is supposed to criticize the child for the response. It is believed that an evaluation-free atmosphere stimulates divergent thinking. In modern times, this method is used in many organizations to generate new and creative solutions.

During the next (red light) stage, evaluation of each alternative is undertaken. Participants discuss the strength and weakness of each solution alternative. In this process, the best alternative is selected and adopted.

It is important to observe that brain storming method presupposes the suspension of critical attitude in the beginning phase. It is asserted that free thinking is essential in the beginning. Subsequently critical thinking may be adopted. A person may take clue from this description and apply in his personal life. A spontaneous generation of alternative solutions followed by a rigorous critical analysis is productive.

Synetics. The other method popularized by psychologists is called synetics. It is other-wise known as analogical thinking. It is observed that "remote association" is involved in creative thinking. For example, Eliot's expression that "the evening is spread like a patient etherized on the table" sounds marvelous. Two seemingly different and distant objects (evening and the etherized patient) are associated to depict the dullness of the evening. In the field of science, Graham Bell invented telephone when he "saw" the similarity between bone of the inner ear and the wire. Similarly, Thomas Young, the physicist, proponent of wave theory of light (which, of course, was subsequently rejected) saw the analogy between two energy sources: water and light.

In the method of synetics (analogy training), psychologists ask participants to imagine similarity between various forms. For example, participants may be asked to imagine themselves as snakes and imagine relevant experience for sometimes. In object analogy, people may be asked to imagine themselves as chairs and meditate on relevant experience for sometime. It is asserted that people find new solutions for problem when they free themselves from fixed and familiar analogy. The possibility of remote association paves the way for creative solution.

Thinking Hat Method. More recently, psychologists have suggested thinking hat method. A simple illustration can be presented here. In a training session, hats of two colours (say, blue and red) are provided. Some participants are asked to put on blue hat whereas others are asked to use red hats. Participants wearing blue hats are asked to speak in favour of a topic while persons with red hats are asked to oppose it. This debate goes on for quite sometime. Then hats are changed and accordingly people are asked to alter their stands. Thus, each person is placed in a condition of thinking both aspects of a single issue. It is argued that this habit of breaking stereotypic thought pattern is helpful in creative process.

In sum, individuals are advised to abandon over-critical attitude (especially at the beginning of a solution-attempt), to stretch imagination for linking the seemingly different ideas and objects, and relinquish the rigidity of prevailing modal thought pattern. These attempts are likely to foster creativity in an individual.

Steps in Creative Production

Creative productions are valued in all societies. It has been posited that the ability to think divergently (in a flexible manner) lies at the root of creative process. Although the importance of divergent thinking is well-accepted in view of its linkage with novelty, one fundamental question requires intelligent response. Is convergent thinking useless from stand-point of creative process?

The convergent thinking is exemplified when a child answers in this way to a question: In how many ways can you use a piece of chalk? The child may answer that a piece of chalk can be used to draw a line, to draw a triangle, to draw a circle, to draw a square, and to draw a rectangle. Although the child expresses five ideas, all are directed to the same goal (thought category) of drawing a geometrical pattern. In other words, the thoughts seem to converge on one point (i.e., drawing a geometrical pattern).

On the contrary, another child may indicate flexibility in thought category. This is called *divergent thinking*. For example, the child may answer that a piece of chalk can be used to draw a line, can be used to drive away a bird, can be used to prevent a leakage in a small hole, can be used to make some marks on a human body, and can be used to make tapping sound on the table. As with the Child 1, here are also five ideas; but these belong to separate thought categories. This is indicative of higher flexibility. This is an expression of divergent thinking, since the thoughts point to different directions.

Although flexibility (thought category) is a better indicator of creativity compared with fluency (amount of thoughts) and divergent thinking has a greater role than convergent thinking, the importance of the latter can not be dismissed altogether. It may not be very useful to start with random search for novelty (Thus engaging oneself in divergent thinking). If one goes to the street and looks for Mr. Novelty in an random manner, the search process may not be successful. On the contrary, it is wiser to start with convergent process. It is also likely that "deviate cases" would be encountered while working in a normative (convergent) manner. In order to find solution for the deviate case, the exploration of the creative individual leads to divergent thinking.

A beautiful illustration can be cited from the life of Alexander Fleming. In accordance with his normative practice (convergent thinking), Fleming conducted some tests. When he got back, he found that virus was destroyed and fungus was formed on the test-tube. Another person in Fleming place might have thought that there was something wrong in his experiment he would have repeated the same experiment. Yet, Fleming took it seriously and made extensive exploration as to why it happened that way. The search process led to the invention of pencillin-a form of antibiotics that revolutionalized the treatment process.

The relative importance of convergent (following a prevailing norm) and divergent thinking is clear when we consider a sequence that characterizes creative process. The process has *four* distinct stages: preparation, exploration, incubation, and evaluation. These stages are common to all forms of creative production such as art, literature, science.

Preparation. This is a stage with which all of us are familiar. The person sets his or her goal and makes preliminary arrangements. Planning is undertaken. Necessary aids are collected. Plans are made and modified. Basically the person engages himself or herself in convergent thinking. At this stage, the mode of convergent thinking (as per the prevailing norm) is more pronounced than divergent thinking.

Exploration. This is a very crucial stage of creative process. The creative persons look for novelty. The person is motivated to think anew. Consequently, convergent thinking loses its intensity and divergent thinking gains momentum. The creative person thinks many permutations and combinations. Thought experiments are carried out both at the mental and physical level. Needless to say, greater is the effective application of divergent thanking, higher is the probability of success at this stage.

Incubation. During the third phase of creativity, the creative person abandons active mode of thought for a while. It is likely that activity and thought processes during exploration phase do not lead to full-scale satisfaction on the part of the person. The poet, for example, may have composed a poem, but he/she is not fully satisfied with it. In scientific problem solving, the scientist has not yet found the perfect solution. In such cases, the creative person gives up creative search for a while and takes up other unrelated work. This is apparently a "no-think" period.

Although this appears to a "no-think" period, there is some form of unconscious mental activity. That's why it is known as incubation period form of activity necessary for hatching eggs. There are many personal anecdotes that illustrate the beauty of this period. It is told that chemist Kekule was not successful in solving the atomic structure of Benzene. Then he gave up the active exploration and tried to forget about his work. Yet, he dreamt of a snake holding its tail in its mouth. All on a sudden the scientist woke up and generated the atomic structure of Benzene in line with the picture of a snake holding its tail in its mouth. Similarly, nuclear mathematician Poin Care had difficulty in solving a mathematical function. Then he gave up his professional work for some time and went on a geological tour. During his tour, he was getting into a bus and the unusual shape of the steps provided clues to him. He got back suddenly and solved the problem. It is shown that incubation is a period of no overt (external) activity, but problem-solving (mental activity) goes on at the unconscious level.

Evaluation. The completion of the creative product leads to the activity of evaluation at the fourth phase. Prior to disseminating the creative product to the external world, the person attempts his/her own personal evaluation. The person may invite his/her spouse, close friends and intimate associates for evaluating the work. It is important to recognize that evaluation is attempted in terms of prevailing norms and standards. Thus, the role of convergent thinking is brought into play.

Sequence and thinking styles	
Stage of Creative Process	Predominant Thought Pattern
I Preparation	Convergent thinking
II Exploration	Divergent thinking
III Incubation	No overt activity and thinking
IV Evaluation	Convergent thinking

Build Your Confidence

Building confidence is a unique skill that can be mastered through systematic efforts. Prior to delineating specific steps for building confidence, it is necessary to distinguish three forms of confidence. First, one type of confidence is very generalized. The person feels that he/she can competently execute a large number of functions. This is a sense of general ability. Although we would expect a person with *generalized confidence* to do a lot of activities competently, we would not expect him or her to jump into water to save a drowning child, if he/she does not know how to swim.

This brings us to a second type of confidence *area-specific confidence*. A person has confidence in the area of music whereas another person has confidence in the area of driving. Similarly, a student may have confidence in the domain of academics while another student may have confidence in the area of physical exercise. This area-specific confidence makes it possible to make accurate prediction. For example, if the academic-confidence (an area-specific confidence) level of a student is known, it is possible to predict his/her academic achievement.

Furthermore, the third type of confidence is called *collective confidence*. It is the confidence level of a group. A team needs to have collective confidence to win a game. All the teachers as a group need to have collective confidence to ensure that the new syllabi would work successfully. Many kinds of social change and social programmes depend on collective confidence of a community.

The most fundamental question involves. What are the techniques of building self-confidence? A number of concrete suggestions can be offered. First, the individual has to expose himself or herself to mastery experiences. Many people do not venture out new experiences. This inhibits self-confidence. On the contrary, people need to go beyond restrictive environment and search for new experiences. The mastery experiences bring new confidence. This is akin to the case of a young boy and girl going to see circus, even if children are scared of big animals at this stage.

Second, it would be very wise to structure initial experience in a particular way. While undertaking a task, some people adopt gambler's attitude and try very difficult tasks. At the other extreme, some people undertake very easy tasks. Both of these approaches are faulty. Too many failures in the beginning bring helplessness and depression. Too many successes in the beginning lower's one's capacity to tolerate frustration later in life. It is also wise to start with tasks of moderate level difficulty. A substantial amount of success, not total success, induces confidence. The person becomes adept to cope with difficult situations later.

Third, the person has to look for a *role model* in the vicinity and follow him or her. Role model is essential. Generally, people encounter role models, but unfortunately they see the "dissimilarity" between the role model and themselves. Because of this perception of dissimilarity, they do not imitate the role model though they admire the role model. It is suggested that they should emphasize the "similarity" between the role model and themselves. They may argue that the role model may be having some advantages, but role model may also have some problems elsewhere. Similarly, they may be having difficulty in some areas but they have advantages elsewhere. This kind of self-persuasion would reduce the perception of dissimilarity and enhance perception of similarity. Between themselves and the role model. Consequently, the person would feel like imitating.

While imitating the role model, the role model would function as a source of information and inspiration. People may observe as to how the role model is talking, behaving and performing. In addition, the role model would provide inspiration to motivate people.

Finally, it is suggested that others can use a lot of social persuasion for building confidence of target persons. Children develop self confidence when parents keep on repeating "you can do it". Similarity, students develop self confidence when teachers repeat "you can do it".

Thus, induction of confidence is not an underealistic phenomenon. The behavioural steps as out-lined above bring positive results surely and steadily.

What is The Level of Your Self-Confidence?

Instruction: Please encircle the number against each statement to indicate the extent of your belief.

	Not at all True	Barely True	Moderately True	Exactly True
1. I always manage to solve difficult problems if I try hard enough.	1	2	3	4
2. If someone opposes me, I can find means and ways to get what I want.	1	2	3	4
3. It is easy for me to stick to my aims and accomplish my goals.	1	2	3	4
4. I am confident that I could deal efficiently with unexpected events.	1	2	3	4
5. Thanks to my resourcefulness, I know how to handle unforeseen Situations.	1	2	3	4
6. I can solve most problems if I invest the necessary effort.	1	2	3	4
7. I remain calm when facing difficulties because I can rely on my coping abilities.	1	2	3	4
8. When I am confronted with a problem I usually find several solutions.	1	2	3	4
9. If I am in a problem, I can usually think of something to do.	1	2	3	4
10. No matter of what comes my way, I'm usually able to handle it.	1	2	3	4

Interpretation

Add your ratings across all ten items. Interpret your score: Below 10: very low confidence.

11-20: Low Self-Confidence

21-30: Moderate Level of Self-Confidence

Above 30: High Self-Confidence

As You Think so You Become

Life is a self-fulfilling prophecy. As we think, so we become. This is not a hear-say. It is based on some experimental research. Psychologists term it *Pygmalion effect*. The word Pygmalion does not carry any dictionary meaning. The world famous play-wright George Bernard Shaw wrote a drama titled "Pygmalion". Pygmalion is the name of a Greek sculptor who made a statue and felt in love with her. Out of compassion for the sculptor, Greek gods brought life to the statue and the sculptor married her.

This Greek imagery has been used by G. B. Shaw for his drama. The drama was subsequently given a film version: "My Fair Lady". In the film, Professor Higgins is a Professor of English Language and Literature. He is with the University of London. As a Professor of Language, he is very particular about people's spoken English. He feels very upset if somebody speaks faulty English, known as cockney English in London.

One beautiful afternoon, Professor Huggins was spending time in a garden in London. He came across a girl selling flowers in the streets of London. Because the girl had a rural background, she was dressed in a rustic way. She was also speaking English in funny ways. However,

Professor Higgins did not get angry. He took fascination in the girl and asked if she was interested to learn English. The girl replied in affirmative Professor Higgins asked the girl to stay in his place and spent a lot of time teaching her English. It continued for weeks and months. There were setbacks. Yet, the coaching continued. The girl grew into a beautiful young woman.

Once she was walking along the street. She met a young man who addressed her "My Fair Lady". This unexpected loving address galvanized her. She said "Young man! You have addressed me as your fair lady. I would be always a fair lady to you. Professor Higgins treated me like a flower girl. I would be a flower girl to him. The difference between a flower girl and a fair lady is not how they are dressed, but how they are behaved".

This is the climax of the story. The film ends with the marriage of the lady and the young-man. But that is not very important. What she says is pregnant with meaning. It clearly imparts a valuable message. The expectation you hold about yourself and others is very important. If you want people to be elevated, you ought to have reasonably high expectation of them. Similarly, if you want to rise, you need to have reasonably high expectation of you. This is *Pygmalion effect* in life.

Interestingly, one psychology professor in Harvard University (USA) took clues and experimented. In two elementary schools of San Francisco, he gave two different kinds of impressions to teachers. In one school, he led teachers to believe that the children were bright. In the other school, he led teachers to believe that children were dull. After a couple of months, the children in the first school displayed 20 point gains in their intelligence level. This was very unusual. But the psychologist demonstrated that there could be Pygmalion effect in children's performance.

Recent surveys have shown that Pygmalion also goes to work organizations. In other words, with positive thoughts about people, we induce in them some motivating and elevating elements. Similarly, our positive thoughts about ourselves induce in us motivating and elevating elements. We may not be consciously aware of the roots of our action. Yet, good thoughts breed good action.

A Land of Hundred Year Young People

Abkhazia is a tiny republic of Georgia (population 516,600), located on the edge of the Black Sea with the Caucasus Mountains to the north. What makes this place so interesting, though, is its "long-living people." In this country, there is no word such as "old" or "elderly" that can be used to describe people. Instead, those who live to be more than 100 years old are called "long-living people." And, although people tend to be very ling-lived in Abkhazia, the region is not filled with frail folks! They stand tall, very few need glasses or false teeth, and most of them do physical labour.

A number of special features characterize that culture. First, there is no such thing as "retirement" in Abkhazia. People keep working for their entire lives, although at a slower pace when they are older. The long-living people work in the fields, do household chores, and tend to livestock. In Abkhazia, over-eating is considered a serious health risk, and overweight people are viewed as ill. In general, the Abkhazian diet is very healthy (lots of vegetables and fruits, very little meat) and people consume fewer calories per day. The low level of stress in this culture is another likely contributor to the longevity of its residents. Competition is frowned upon, and moderation in everything is highly valued. It is not surprising that many people in abkhazia are "long-living".

This country of hundred years young demonstrates two salient factors. First, good health habits are important. It has been demonstrated again and again that most of the modern diseases are the product of faulty life style changes. Smoking, drug-addition, alcoholism and lack of proper rest are some of causal factors of contemporary illness.

Second, management of stress is essential. While handling stress it is important to point out that there are two basic modalities of management: *preventive strategy and curative strategy*. Furthermore, preventive strategy is more helpful than curative strategy. This preventive strategy includes steps that are taken prior to the on-set of stressors. While curative strategy is adopted following stress responses. It is axiomatic to assert that prevention is better than cure.

Will to Live

An incredible story about Felipe Garza was reported. Felipe was a 15-year-old boy living in California (USA). He fell in love with a 14-year-old named Donna. With echoes of Romeo Juliet, it soon developed that Donna was dying of degenerative heart disease. Felype had the benefit of good health. He went to his mother and told her that when he died, he wanted Donna to have his heart.

Less than a month later, Felipe suffered a burst blood vessel in the brain and died. As he expressed, his heart was transplanted in his girl-friend Donna by surgeons in San Francisco. Except for some minor investigation of cases of volunteer death, no one has studied the idea of a "will to die". It is not certainty apparent how a teenager could will himself to stroke. Puzzling cases like Felipe Gaza are useful in stretching our thinking on these issues. Conversely is it possible that people can prolong their lives by "will to live"?

Although there are not many systematic studies on the issue of willing to live", health psychologists have identified a personality cluster called *self-healing personality*. The case of Mahatma Gandhi is the finest example of self-healing personality. He was not sickly, although he spent over 2,300 days in prison and endured numerous self-imposed fasts. On the contrary, he had the personal strength and commitment to be one of the most influential leaders of the 20th century, and perhaps, of all times. He pioneered nonviolent political resistance, instituted numerous social reforms and political freedom for India.

In a small measure Noam Sharansky, the Jewish social activist is another exampling character. He was convicted of treason in Moscow and was sentenced to many years at hard labour. His real crime was that he was an activist who was trying to emigrate to Israel from the former Soviet Union. At the end of the trial, Sharansky stood up in the court and said "I have no regrets. I am happy, I am happy and I lived honesty, in peace with my conscience". Sharansky survived many years in Soviet Union and was eventually permitted to emigrate to Israel, in good health. White waiting, he did what he could, with help from his wife.

The case studies of Gandhi, Sharansky and other self-healing personalities illustrate the role of commitment in life. It is not the commitment to self-improvement, rather commitment to objectives larger than life. What defined Gandhiji's life was a commitment to principle. Various studies document that alienation is unhealthy. Obligation and dedication are healthy. Some people find this commitment in religion; others in philosophy; other people seek political reform. Some people simply have a hobby. What they have in common is a sense of purpose.

It is important to recognize that commitment to something needs to be important and meaningful. Many competitive Japanese are now working longer and longer hours with a consuming passion. Yet, the result is not unmixed. They now are concerned about sudden death and death from overwork.

What is needed in addition to commitment is a spirit of *enthusiasm*. The word enthusiasm literally means "having a godly spirit within" *Cheerfulness* is another good emotional term. Deriving from the word for "face", cheer at one time referred people express good spirits through their faces. Several good clues indicate emotional balance and the inherent resilience are key factors. The "will to live" is not a static process. It originates, grows or spreads its positive effects all around.

Smile and Stay Happy

People infer what they think or how they feel by observing their own behaviour and the situation in which it takes place. Think about it. Have you ever listened to yourself argue with somebody, only to realize with amazement how angry you were? Have you ever finished your meal in record time, only then to conclude that you must have been very hungry. In each case, you make an inference about yourself by watching your own behaviour.

Of course, there are limits to self-perception. People do not infer their own internal states from behaviour that occurred in the presence of compelling situational pressures. For example, a person would not infer that he/she is happy when he/she is singing a song with the promise of a reword or incentive. But the person would make such inference when he/she is going along the road and singing a song. Similarly, a student may not infer about his/her interest if asked by his/her professor to make a presentation. On the contrary, he/she would infer about his/her interest in the topic if he/she talking about it without provocation.

Viewed from the standpoint of such self-perception, it is posited that changes in facial expression can trigger corresponding changes in the subjective experience of emotion. In a study, participants were told that they were taking part in an experiment on activity of the facial muscle. After attaching electrodes to their faces, the investigator showed them a series of cartoons. Before each one, the participants were instructed to contract certain facial muscles in ways that created either a smile or a frown. As expected, participants rated what they saw as funnier, and reported feeling happier, when they were smiling than when they were frowning.

It is possible that facial expressions affect emotion through a process of self-perception. "If I am smiling, I must be happy".

Consistent with this expectation, people were asked to emulate either the happy or angry facial expression that were depicted in a series of photographs. Half of the participants saw themselves in a mirror during this task, the others did not. Compared to participants in a no-expression group, those who put on happy faces felt better and those who put on angry faces felt worse. Moreover, these differences were particularly pronounced among participants who saw themselves in a mirror.

Other researchers maintain that facial movements spark emotion by producing physiological changes in the brain. For example, smiling causes facial muscles to increase the flow of air-cooled blood to the brain. This process produces a pleasant state by lowering brain temperature. Conversely, frowning increases blood flow, producing an unpleasant state by raising temperature.

Other expressive behaviours such as body postures can also provide feedback and influence the way we feel. When people feel proud, they stand erect with their shoulders raised, chest expanded and head held high. When dejected, people slump over their shoulders, drooping, and head bowed. Clearly your emotional state is revealed in the way you carry yourself.

It is also possible that the way you carry yourself affects your emotional state. You can lift your spirit by expansion. You can lift your legs while walking and feel happy. Thus, the relationship between emotion and physical gesture is not a one-way traffic. You can produce positive emotional states (such as happiness, smartness) by adopting appropriate physical posture. You smile and feel happy, you walk bravely and feel smart.

■

Books Authored by F.M. Sahoo

- Cognitive styles and amp; interpersonal behaviour
- Affective sensitivity and amp; cognitive styles
- Psychology in Indian context (Edited)
- Environment and amp; behaviour
- Child rearing and amp; educating assistance manual
- Dynamics of human helplessness
- Sex roles in transition
- Behavioural issues in ageing (Edited)
- Atlas of mind
- Mysteries of mind
- Wonders of mind
- Splendours of mind
- Mind management
- Tools of mind
- Landscape of mind
- Plasticity of mind
- Melody of Minds
- Happiness flows
- Dynamics of Personal Growth
- Essentials of Employee Counselling
- Dynamics of Personal Growth
- A Passage to Neuroscience of Leadership
- Close of Mind

Books in Odia

- Bichitra mana
- Manasika bikruti
- Jiban prabahare manasika bikruti
- Adhuni ka jibanare manasika chapa
- Manara manachitra
- Manastatvika bikasare saisaba parba
- Byaktitva & amp; netrutva
- Nari manastatva
- Manastatvika bikasara godhuli parba
- Sisu manara bigyan
- Sachitra mana
- Sabala mana, saphala jibana
- Manastatvika bikasara balya parba
- Manastatvika bikasara kaishore parba
- Manasika samasya O samadhan
- Manara rahasya
- Jibana O' manastatwa
- Tallinata
- Sahitya O' Manastatwa
- Chapamukta jeeban
- Sakshyatakara
- Manastatwika Bikashar Jouban Parba
- Sukhanubhutira Marmakatha
- Mana Prikrama
- Manara Bhugola
- Mana Paribhasa-1
- Purnatara Pandulipi
- Sri SatyaSai Gitikavya
- Baibhava Manobigyan

Translation

- Divya Sambasana (Part-v)
- Divya Sambasana (Part-xv)
- Shiridi ru Puttaparti
- Siksha Samparkare
- Bibeka Sampritee
- Chetanadipta Jiban
- Dhyanadipta Jiban

Black Eagle Books

www.blackeaglebooks.org
info@blackeaglebooks.org

Black Eagle Books, an independent publisher, was founded as a nonprofit organization in April, 2019. It is our mission to connect and engage the Indian diaspora and the world at large with the best of works of world literature published on a collaborative platform, with special emphasis on foregrounding Contemporary Classics and New Writing.

www.ingramcontent.com/pod-product-compliance
Lightning Source LLC
Chambersburg PA
CBHW060607080526
44585CB00013B/711